}

FINANCE AND INVESTMENT

UNIT 5

PROJECT APPRAISAL

MBA

Financial Strategy

Prepared for the Course Team by Jan Gadella
and Janette Rutterford

The Open University
BUSINESS SCHOOL

OPEN UNIVERSITY COURSE TEAM

Core Group

Professor Janette Rutterford, *Production and Presentation Course Team Co-Chair and Author*

Bernardo Bátiz-Lazo, *Presentation Course Team Co-Chair and Author*

Marcus Davison, *Author*

Graham Francis, *Author*

Carmel de Nahlik

Jan Gadella, *Author*

Margaret Greenwood

Heinz Kassier

Karen Kingsnorth, *Course Manager*

Clare Minchington, *Author and 99K Presentation Chair*

Pat Sucher, *Author*

Patricia Swannell, *Author*

Richard Wheatcroft, *Author*

External Assessor

Professor Paul Draper, *Walter Scott and Partners Professor of Finance, University of Edinburgh*

Production Team

Sylvan Bentley, *Picture Researcher*

John Bradley, *Design Group Co-ordinator*

Martin Brazier, *Graphic Designer*

Henry Dougherty, *Editor*

Jenny Edwards, *Product Quality Assistant*

Anne Faulkner, *Information Specialist*

John Garne, *Computing Consultant*

Roy Lawrance, *Graphic Artist*

David Libbert, *BBC Series Producer*

Richard Mole, *Director of Production OUBS*

Kathy Reay, *Course Team Assistant*

Linda K. Smith, *Project Controller*

Doreen Tucker, *Compositor*

Steve Wilkinson, *BBC Series Producer*

External Critical Readers

Stephen Abbott

George Buckberry

Linda Cinderey

Roland Davis

Angela Garrett

Jane Hughes

Ed Hutt

Rosemary F. Johnson

Geoff Jones

Robin Joy

David Kirk

Archie McArthur

Richard Mischak

Professor Chris Napier

Eugene Power

Manvinder Singh

Tony Whitford

The Open University, Walton Hall, Milton Keynes MK7 6AA

First published 1998. Second edition 1999. Third edition 2000. Reprinted 2001, 2002

Copyright © 1998, 1999, 2000 The Open University

Edited, designed and typeset by The Open University

Printed in the United Kingdom by The Burlington Press, Foxton, Cambridge CB2 6SW.

ISBN 0 7492 9729 X

Further information on Open University Business School courses may be obtained from the Course Sales Development Centre, The Open University, PO Box 222, Milton Keynes MK7 6YY (Telephone: 01908 653449).

3.3

24945B/b821b3u5i3.3

CONTENTS

1 INTRODUCTION

The importance of capital investments cannot be overemphasised. Investments affect the operations and cash flows of organisations over long periods of time. However, capital investment *per se* does not necessarily improve organisational performance: success depends upon how efficiently and effectively capital resources are used. Organisations frequently spend large amounts of money on capital investments which may only give returns after a long period of time, and this increases the degree of uncertainty for the returns on these investments. Moreover, an organisation's capital resources are usually limited. Consequently, the resource allocation decision is often critical to the organisation's success.

The process of making a capital expenditure (CAPEX) decision is a multifunctional undertaking. In most cases this process involves people in a range of functions within the organisation. Each of them provides input according to the type of project under consideration and their individual expertise.

To clarify the issues described in this unit we make use of a range of case studies. These will form the basis for explaining theory and provide means for illustrating the practical issues.

To accommodate the requirements of students in the governmental and not-for-profit sectors we will examine appraisal issues in the UK National Health Service (NHS). We shall also devote a section to Public Private Partnerships (PPP), and to the Private Finance Initiative (PFI) in particular. We will also attempt to illustrate the link between capital expenditure and balance sheet structure, because the topics dealing with capital expenditure are not 'stand alone' subjects. We are dealing with a holistic process, where one action impacts upon others which affect activities and processes throughout the organisation. However, this subject will be discussed in greater depth in Unit 6, Company Appraisal.

Holistic: tending to produce wholes from the grouping of structures.

The procedure of project appraisal also requires a consideration of risk, and Block 4 of B821, which focuses on risk, will elaborate some of the issues discussed in this Unit.

Some of the functional areas involved in the capital investment decision are:

- *marketing* – it provides data estimates of sales volumes if, for example, the proposed investment is for a facility to produce new products
- *production* – it can determine the use of scarce resources in the manufacture of the organisational output
- *services* – departments, institutions, divisions and similar functional areas responsible for providing services (e.g. schools, department of transport)
- *accounting and finance* – it can provide data needed for the analysis of the project and the expertise to carry out quantitative analysis upon which the decision to invest is based. This function examines methods of financing capital investment projects and estimates their effect on cash flows, taxes and profitability.

Management must recognise and integrate the decision-making process within the organisational environment and select the projects that meet the chosen investment criteria in order to achieve the strategic and operational objectives of the organisation.

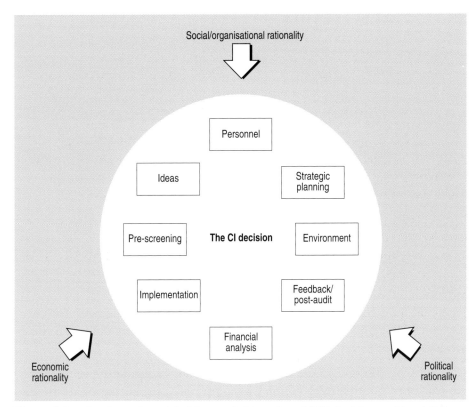

Figure 1.1   A universal model of the capital investment (CI) decision-making activity (Northcott, 1992)

The model in Figure 1.1 shows a range of factors which influence the decision to invest in capital projects. The level of influence these factors have on the investment process varies between different types of organisations, and may vary to a certain extent between different projects within one organisation. The principal purpose of the model is to illustrate the complexity of the decision-making process and the range of expertise which is needed to arrive at a reasonable investment decision. The three arrows symbolise the external influences on the decision-making process, and of course these vary according to the type of organisation as well as the individual project.

Outline of Unit 5

The structure of this unit will be as follows. Section 2, 'Strategy and investment appraisal', illustrates the importance of strategy in the capital investment decision-making process. Although this subject has already been examined in Units 1 and 2, it will be revisited in this unit.

In Section 3, 'Techniques of investment appraisal', we explore a range of issues in connection with techniques of investment appraisal and the principles of capital budgeting. This section uses a case study based on London Transport. This organisation is obliged to spend many millions of pounds per year in order to sustain and improve the underground and bus system in the London conurbation. The case provides an illustration of how management conduct investment decision-making processes in large public organisations which, although they derive most of their revenue from customers, have social, political and economic motives other than profit or shareholder wealth maximisation. The section also describes specific issues closely intertwined with investment appraisal, such as inflation and taxation. As organisations become increasingly multinational, a significant portion of their capital expenditure is directed abroad. Specific appraisal problems deriving from international investment programmes are also dealt with in this section.

Risk issues in CAPEX are discussed in Section 4. In this section we also describe the so-called 'options' approach to capital investment, which is a relatively new approach to the process of project decision-making. This development is a valuable tool enabling organisations to manage and control risk.

In Section 5, 'Funding capital projects', we introduce the subject of leasing, which has been for a number of years an important finance mechanism for a range of plant and equipment investments. This section also deals with project finance. This type of financing is becoming increasingly popular for funding large capital projects, such as power stations, oil refineries, etc. To illustrate the opportunities and complexities of project finance, we look at a case study of how a large bank views a capital investment in a liquid gas facility in Oman. In Section 5, we also consider the funding of capital projects and their importance in the overall corporate capital structure, as discussed in Unit 4. We introduce the Private Finance Initiative, a mechanism to allow public-sector organisations in the UK to use the private sector to fund public-sector projects.

Section 6, 'Capital rationing', builds on the issues of funding and explains the concept of capital rationing in a commercial context. This section also deals with issues surrounding competing projects. Nearly all organisations are subject to spending constraints and management may have to choose between various projects for investment. This is equally true in the public sector where decisions are also affected by groups other than management such as electors, politicians, pressure groups, government officials and experts.

In Section 7 you are asked to attempt a spreadsheet exercise. The task requires careful consideration of the aspects of CAPEX you will have covered in the unit and you will be able to practise working with Excel spreadsheets. The accompanying disk provides you with a suggested solution to the exercise.

Aims and objectives of the unit

By the end of this unit you should be able to:
- appreciate how organisations implement their capital appraisal procedures
- recognise the wide range of issues involved in capital investment decisions
- assess the strategic implications of investing in capital equipment and facilities
- apply a range of project appraisal methods to various types of projects and organisations in which CAPEX decisions are made
- appreciate the importance of, and the problems of identifying and measuring, risk in the context of capital investment decision making
- understand the problems and opportunities of raising funds for capital projects in the market-place
- undertake the investment appraisal exercise at the end of this unit.

2 STRATEGY AND INVESTMENT APPRAISAL

In this section we consider the need to appreciate the role of organisational strategy in the capital investment process. This topic has already been discussed in Unit 1 (Section 1.3) and Unit 2 (Section 2). However, here we address the topic in the context of CAPEX only. This is particularly relevant as strategy is held to emanate from an overall mission statement, or configuration of objectives and policies, designed to bring about a long-term optimal future for the organisation. CAPEX, by its very nature, has long-term implications for the organisation undertaking such projects. Despite the fact that an individual project may not require expenditure which is substantial in the context of an organisation's total expenditure, strategic considerations should always be incorporated in the decision-making process.

It can be argued that strategy is mainly concerned with adjusting to the opportunities and changes in the business environment. However, strategy also has to be determined within the constraints of the organisation's resources, or such resources as can be obtained. From this it follows that expenditure on capital projects must be integrally linked to these resources.

In general, strategy is understood to encompass the decisions made by governing bodies, senior management and persons who occupy similar positions in government and not-for-profit organisations (e.g. senior clinicians in hospital, senior officers in the armed forces) concerning the long-term relationship between the organisation and its environment. These decisions tend to be of a top-down nature. Strategy attempts to answer such questions as: What business should we be in? What course of action should we pursue? What is the optimal organisation–environment 'fit'? How can the organisation remain flexible? Strategic planning attempts to identify an operational environment in which the organisation has real competitive advantages. In the business sector, many large conglomerates have divested profitable divisions from their portfolios, thus forgoing opportunities, just because these particular operations did not fit into the overall group profile. In the government sector, post World War II strategies of economic intervention and in-house provision of services have now given way to more market-oriented policies and to the outsourcing of services. Many activities previously carried out by government have passed to the private sector via privatisation.

In contrast, a capital project proposal typically follows a bottom-up approach. For example, software engineers may have developed a new product and, in order to produce this, new capital equipment is needed. The engineers prepare a project proposal for appraisal and this proposal then winds its way up the corporate hierarchy to its point of sanctioning. What has happened in this instance is that the engineers proposed their own project without necessarily having in mind, or indeed knowing, the overall organisational long-term direction. The final decision on this particular capital project proposal will reflect strategic choices made by senior management and, if the software product project does not 'fit' into the desired category, it will not go forward for implementation.

So, capital investment decision-making forms part of the wider strategic process. Capital projects should not be viewed in isolation, but within the overall environment, the organisation's goals and its strategic direction. As a result, during the initiation of a project, its sponsors or their managers should answer such questions as:

- Is the proposal compatible with organisational strategy?
- Is the idea technically feasible?
- Do we have access to the required resources (finance, technology, skills)?

Strategic and financial appraisals should be linked when longer-term financial decisions are being made. Management need a framework in which to consider strategic as well as financial issues. Some factors to be considered are:

- When is a long-term financial investment decision strategic?
- What are the links between strategic and financial appraisal?

2.1 EXAMPLE OF STRATEGIC AND FINANCIAL APPRAISAL

In order to illustrate the importance of strategy in the CAPEX decision-making process read Box 2.1.

BOX 2.1   CASE STUDY: W.H. SMITH INVESTMENT IN RETAIL STORES

The senior managers of W.H. Smith are of the opinion that its strength lies in its expertise in retail marketing. As a result, corporate strategy is focused on the maximisation of returns from retail outlets. For example, one of their objectives is to maintain market share in the UK book market at 25%. To achieve this the company opened an additional 60,000 sq. feet of retail outlet space per year during the 1980s and this tactic allowed them to attain the desired sales targets. However, during the 1990s, a new trend of retailing emerged: large out-of-town shopping complexes became fashionable and the environment of retailing changed accordingly.

The development financing of these out-of-town shopping complexes is based on guaranteed cash flows from retailers, and so, during the planning stages, the principal UK retailers, such as Marks & Spencer, Burton's, Body Shop and W.H. Smith, are canvassed for their potential interest in each new development. If these firms are interested in supporting a new shopping complex, they are offered certain incentives to obtain their commitment, such as the selection of shop locations of their choice, certain leasing advantages and so on. As a major High Street retailer, W.H. Smith is always invited to take part in these schemes.

During the early 1990s a new development was mooted near London in East Thurrock, to be called Lakeside, just north of the Dartford Thames tunnel and new bridge, off the M25 motorway. This was to be a vast shopping complex, even larger than the Metro complex in Newcastle upon Tyne which was at the time claimed to be the largest in Europe.

However, W.H. Smith had recently invested in shops in smaller complexes closer to London, in the proximity of the new proposed complex. In other words, the new complex was going to be situated in the existing catchment area of the 'newish' outlets. As a result the revenue of these outlets would certainly be reduced if Lakeside were to go ahead. What was the W.H. Smith management to do? Not to participate in the new scheme would provide the opposition, for example John Menzies, with the opportunity to open a store in Lakeside, causing W.H. Smith to lose market share. However, participation would entail loss of custom for their existing stores to the benefit of the new store.

It could be argued, and presumably management did take that viewpoint, that not to invest would mean reducing the customer-base of their existing stores anyway because the competitors would move into Lakeside as an alternative to W.H. Smith.

The final result was that W.H. Smith participated in the Lakeside project which has proved to be a successful retail project with people coming from far and wide to shop there, with sales more than compensating for lost sales at other W.H. Smith stores.

In the final analysis, the corporate strategy of W.H. Smith drove the CAPEX decision-making process and, despite some worries about its performance during the middle 1990s, W.H. Smith still has the brand name of a solid and reliable supplier of its product range.

The W.H. Smith case study illustrates the point that the capital project investment strategy must, by its very essence, be linked to the strategy of the organisation. Management should never overlook this link or focus their attention entirely on the investment decision.

If we examine the role of CAPEX further, and adopt a wider perspective, we can see that strategy in effect drives the whole process of investing in capital assets.

2.2 THE CAPITAL INVESTMENT (CI) MODEL

The model illustrated in Figure 2.1 is only an approximation of the effects of strategy on the decision-making process but it does highlight the dominant position of strategic factors in this process. This model mirrors the method by which W.H. Smith evaluates its investment in retail stores,

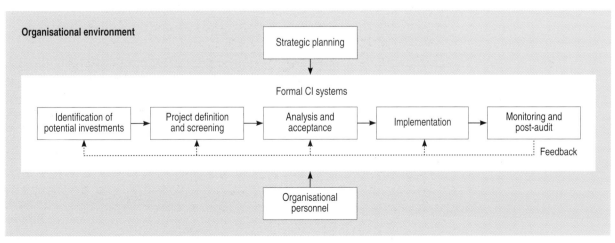

Figure 2.1 Capital investment (CI) model, highlighting the influence of strategy on the process (Maccarone, 1996)

as described in Box 2.1. The capital investment (CI) process is depicted as occurring within the context of the organisational environment, although the exact nature of interactions between capital investments and other functional areas in the organisation may be unclear.

The process of investment appraisal is often viewed as separate from other activities in the organisation, such as operating procedures and systems. However, the model shows that the CAPEX activities should be integrated and linked to the strategic planning process. The formal organisational factors, planning process and investment characteristics are strictly interconnected. Many investment decisions can have a significant impact on the organisation as a whole, and on its long-term performance, hence they must be considered as strategic decisions.

Finally, it could be argued that concentration on investment appraisal techniques such as NPV and IRR, which are discussed in more detail in Section 3, may have been overdone, particularly with the wide use and understanding of spreadsheets. Organisations might do better by paying more attention to reviewing their CAPEX programmes within the wider strategic context. This view was reinforced by a business commentator in the *Financial Times* who commented that:

> This [concentration on a strategic approach to investment appraisal] has in fact occurred due to pressure applied by large fund managers on the conglomerates which originated in the 1970s and 1980s. And as a result the pendulum has now swung back to the investment in viable projects within a strategic plan.

Financial Times 7 July 1997

Activity 2.1

Examine a project or programme proposal recently adopted by an organisation in which you work or otherwise participate. Try to outline the decision process the project went through. The following series of questions to address to your fellow organisation participants may prove a useful tool in doing this.

How is programming carried out?

How do you get involved? How would you describe the role you play?

How much is at stake in the process? How much effort goes into the process?

How does the process stand in relation to strategic planning?

How does the programme proposal document relate the proposed new programme to the organisation's goals and objectives?

How does the document describe the likely effect of the proposal on the activities of the organisation?

How does the document deal with the timescale for proposal implementation and impact?

How much evidence does the document provide about the proposal's feasibility? How does the document deal with risk and uncertainty?

How much money and/or other resources does the document indicate would be involved if the proposal went ahead?

To what extent was the programme proposal subjected to benefit-cost analysis? Which quantitative techniques were used to evaluate it, if any?

SUMMARY

In this section we have concentrated on strategic issues in CAPEX decisions. Other units in B821 refer to the role of strategy in finance and you should have a good grasp of the subject from your earlier studies. The general consensus is that long-term strategic planning attempts to ensure that an organisation meets its objectives. The results of strategic decisions are interlinked with the wide range of factors which impinge on the business and economic environment. The direct effects of one decision cannot be viewed in isolation as, in most cases, it generates 'domino effects' elsewhere in the organisation and/or related fields of operation. The W.H. Smith example illustrated the strategic considerations involved in determining its project investment portfolio, and the level of strategic discourse management should have before proceeding with a project proposal.

3 Techniques of Investment Appraisal

In this section, we place the process of capital budgeting into the context of organisational practice. We also explore the range of appraisal methods used by organisations.

In order to illustrate the decision-making process in practice, a case study on London Transport describes how a large public-sector organisation undertakes its capital investment programme.

Because inflation and taxation are important factors in the process of financial appraisal, they are briefly discussed in the context of CAPEX.

Finally, as many organisations operate in an international environment, we review aspects of capital budgeting specific to international projects.

3.1 CAPITAL BUDGETING

Capital budgeting is a widely used term for the process of evaluating investments in capital projects. These projects may account for a significant proportion of the total assets of an organisation. In addition, the decision to invest, or not to invest, in capital projects may have a major impact on the financing of the organisation. Expenditure on assets requires management to make decisions about where and in what form to raise funds. A wise acquisition of capital assets together with appropriate funding of those assets can often mean the difference between a business that is competitively strong, with opportunities for growth and market expansion, and a business that is weak and uncompetitive; and, in the non-profit sector, an organisation delivering high quality services that are responding to public need, and an organisation that is ineffective and whose assets are more akin to a liability on the public purse.

The purpose of capital budgeting is to provide policy makers and management with a sound quantitative basis on which to base a capital investment decision. The range of possible investments includes expenditure on buildings, equipment, land, research and development, information technology, changes in stock levels, shares, retail outlets, hotels, roads, railways, coastal defences, mental health institutions and so on. Which particular types of expenditure are considered depends entirely on which type of organisation is planning the investment.

When an investment is made, a cash outlay is exchanged for benefits to be realised in the future in terms of cash or services for public consumption. Proposed investment projects should be judged by their expected return. In this context a number of questions must be asked which form the core of the capital investment decision. Will a particular investment meet the requirements of investors, electors or members? Is the probable profile of cash or service satisfaction inflows v. outflows good enough to meet certain investment criteria? What should those criteria be? Will the effect of an investment decision be a gain to the company's share price (or, in the not-for-profit sector, an increase in, say, customer satisfaction)?

In the commercial sector each proposed project is appraised in terms of the future cash flows that are generated by the investment in the project. The evaluation typically involves both the timing of returns and costs and the application of an appropriate **cost of capital (COC)** as the discount rate. Cash flow items are discounted according to their distance from the present and the rate of discount is applied to *all* changes in revenues and costs (including tax) that will occur if the project proceeds. In practice, qualitative factors, as we saw earlier, may also carry weight in the decision-making process.

> The cost of capital (COC) is the return required by investors in the organisation (this is also known as the weighted average cost of capital, or WACC, defined in Unit 4).

Management aim to select investment projects that will help the organisation to achieve its objectives, providing a reasonable rate of return on invested capital. Indeed, for privately owned companies, it may be expressed explicitly in terms of the maximisation of shareholder value. Management need to determine whether the activities in which they wish to engage are worth the investments and which assets should be required to promote those activities. In the service-oriented public sector, objectives are less easy to express in a financial way, but cost-benefit comparisons may be one way of evaluating proposals.

For each investment proposal, senior management typically require that the expected future cash flows be supported by detailed economic, competitive and technical analyses. The quality of financial forecasts is no better than the assumptions used in their preparation. Hence the need to appreciate and challenge these assumptions and for managers to consider a range of questions such as: Do they make business sense? What would our forecasts look like on different assumptions? Does the project fit the organisational strategy?

Finally, decision-makers must be aware that certain costs do not necessarily involve a cash outlay but involve an opportunity cost. If a currently unused building is to be part of a project and it can be sold now for £3m, net of tax, that amount should be treated as a cash outlay (albeit an opportunity cost) at the outset of the project.

Section 4 of *Vital Statistics* describes the most commonly used capital budgeting appraisal techniques in more detail. These are: net present value (NPV), the internal rate of return (IRR), payback, the accounting rate of return (ARR) and the profitability index (PI). In public sector services, where costs are often more significant than user revenues, a common practice is to calculate the equivalent annual charge of a project. This involves converting the annual capital outlay, or expenditure on fixed assets, to an annual amount. The annual amount is equal to the interest and principal repayments on an instalment loan repayable over the economic life of the assets at the cost of capital prevailing when the project would proceed. This annual charge is added to the annual operating costs of the project (e.g. staff, materials, administration) and the total annual cost is compared with the quantity and quality of the services and other benefits generated by the project each year. Politicians must make the subjective judgement as to whether the "value" of the *annual* benefits exceed the annual costs. No doubt they weigh up various political and social priorities and the effect of their decisions on public opinion.

Each of these appraisal techniques is based on certain assumptions and, therefore, has certain limitations. To compensate for these limitations, many organisations use more than one evaluation method. In the next section, we will see how organisations use these different capital budgeting techniqes in practice.

3.2 ISSUES IN APPRAISAL TECHNIQUES

It is useful at this stage to briefly summarise the reasons for the use of the various financial appraisal methods as well as give a word of caution to the users:

- NPV is theoretically the best method because:
    - (i) it takes account of the time value of money
    - (ii) it depends solely on the forecast cash flows of the projects, and the discount rate which should be used is the cost of capital
    - (iii) since present values are all measured in today's monetary values (sterling, dollars, etc.), they can be added up. The alternative methods do not have this additive property.

- IRR appears to be the appraisal method preferred by practitioners, because it is seen to provide an 'instant' indication of the rate of return or yield on the invested capital. However, there is no wholly satisfactory way of defining the true rate of return of a long-term asset (Brealey and Myers, 1996).

- Firms still use payback because it is easy to calculate when the initial investment outlay has been recovered by the project's cash inflows. This approach may encourage 'short-termism', since the faster the project pays back, the better it is deemed to be. However, although many firms use payback as a quick way to measure the return on capital, in most cases the payback method is applied in tandem with a DCF appraisal technique.

No matter which method of appraisal is applied, the users must be aware of its strengths as well as its shortcomings. After all, it has been said that in appraising capital projects one 'applies exact numbers to uncertain future events'. If we take that into account we must certainly be aware of the fact that numbers alone do not provide a satisfactory answer for considering a capital investment and that in many cases qualitative factors are major influences in the project appraisal process. This is perhaps more obvious in the public sector where profitability criteria are difficult to apply and where democracy is very much part of the decision-making process.

Capital investment processes have been the subject of many studies. Most of them have concentrated on the types of appraisal techniques used, for example Pike (1996), Wilkes, Samuels and Greenfield (1996) and Drury and Tayles (1997).

Activity 3.1 _____
Study Tables 3.1, 3.2 and 3.3 (opposite), derived from a survey of appraisal techniques by Drury and Tayles (1997) and examine the frequency of use of the various appraisal methods and their ranking in perceived importance by the users of these methods.

Table 3.1 Extent of use of investment appraisal techniques			
	Never/rarely (%)	Sometimes (%)	Often/always (%)
Payback method	23	14	63
Accounting return on capital employed	39	20	41
Internal rate of return	32	11	57
Net present value	41	16	43

Table 3.2 Use of different appraisal methods			
	All organisations $n = 278$ (%)	Small organisations $n = 43$ (%)	Larger organisations $n = 46$ (%)
Payback (unadjusted)	63	56	55
Accounting return on capital employed	41	35	53
Internal rate of return*	57	30	85
Net present value*	43	23	80

Indicates that the responses from the small and large organisations are significantly different using the Mann-Whitney U Test at the 1 per cent significance level

Table 3.3 Ranking of investment appraisal techniques			
	All organisations $n = 278$	Small organisations $n = 43$	Larger organisations $n = 46$
Payback (unadjusted)	1.94	1.52	2.49
Accounting return on capital employed	3.17	2.79	3.27
Internal rate of return*	2.32	2.77	1.77
Net present value*	3.08	3.59	2.78
Intuitive managerial judgement	3.15	2.48	3.60

Note: 1 = most important; 5 = least important

Source: Drury and Tayles (1997)

Studies on the use of CAPEX appraisal methods tend to show survey results of organisations of a similar size, e.g. only large companies. However, the Drury and Tayles survey reports findings based on a wide range of companies of different sizes.

Table 3.1 shows that the payback appraisal technique is still popular, despite the problems with that approach. Table 3.2 shows a summary of the replies for those respondents who stated that their firms often or always use a specific technique. The NPV and IRR *appraisal methods are primarily used by larger companies. The research also shows that most respondent organisations use a combination of appraisal techniques.*

Table 3.3 shows the average ranking of the relative importance of the various appraisal methods. The table shows that payback is ranked as the most important technique and IRR as the second most important. However, there was a significant difference between the responses of the larger and smaller companies. The larger ones predominantly ranked IRR as their most frequently used appraisal technique. Payback ranked as the second most important method but the use of intuitive judgement as the least important. In contrast, smaller companies ranked payback as the most important technique. It is not clear why IRR is more frequently used than NPV. The popular view (Pike, 1996) is that academics prefer NPV while practitioners and managers have a preference for IRR, which can more easily be related to a rate of return.

The lower rankings given to intuitive management judgement by larger organisations may be due to the typical requirement for major projects to be submitted to a top management board for formal sanctioning. Larger organisations tend to rely more extensively on formal capital budgeting procedures.

The more frequent use of judgemental intuition by smaller organisations may be because the people who make the decisions have a detailed knowledge of the projects and may place less emphasis on the financial appraisal process. In these conditions they are more likely to base their decisions on knowledge of the business.

Surveys have also highlighted that the CAPEX process is normally a bottom-up procedure (see Section 2.1). However, when large capital-intensive projects are proposed the process is normally reversed and a top-down (proposals initiated by top-management) procedure applies. This last category tends to confirm what was suggested in Section 2.1 – that strategic issues do have an impact on major CAPEX decisions.

Nevertheless, such surveys may give too favourable and rational a picture of organisational CAPEX practices. For instance, although managers may use DCF techniques, this does not mean that decision-makers place great emphasis on the results. It is not clear what impact positive project cash flow profiles have on the decision-making process. In fact, it is not even obvious who makes the CAPEX decisions and what role top management plays in capital budgeting processes (Pike, 1996).

Studies (Pike, 1996) have revealed that a superior/manager supports those projects which are in his or her interest to undertake (possibly not such a great discovery!). Authors such as Pike have also noted that the capital budgeting process may be influenced less by financial than by other factors.

Lumijärvi (1992) suggests that, even for large organisations, the CAPEX process may be a mere ritual. This could mean that lower-level managers/project sponsors submit only project proposals which are likely to be approved. If a proposal is rejected, a subordinate could face embarrassment and a loss of face. Lumijärvi also notes that investment decisions are the result of sequential bargaining at different organisational levels. More precisely, between the initiation and final approval of an investment, different people and groups bargain. During bargaining people commit themselves to the projects, making it increasingly more difficult to cancel or reject the proposals. As the CAPEX proposal travels up the corporate hierarchy towards its point of sanctioning it gathers political support and momentum along the way. In this context Lumijärvi suggests that 'a capital investment calculation is not the most important determinant in the final decision-making'.

Activity 3.2

For a more detailed discussion of the CAPEX process, read the article by Lumijärvi, entitled 'Selling of capital investments to top management', in the Course Reader. This describes how the CAPEX process evolves in a large Scandinavian firm.

3.3 LONDON TRANSPORT CASE STUDY

Introduction

London Transport (LT) is responsible for operating the Underground train and bus network in London. The Underground system is operated under the 1984 Transport Act, which requires that LT provide, with the available resources, the best possible network for transportation. One of the major difficulties that management face is how to allocate scarce resources for the Underground system and other services. Managers must determine operating objectives to maximise the social benefits to the community and accordingly a range of objectives must be considered such as: What transport needs do we have to meet? What levels of service must we provide through trains? How do we decide whether, for example, south London needs an improved Underground service?

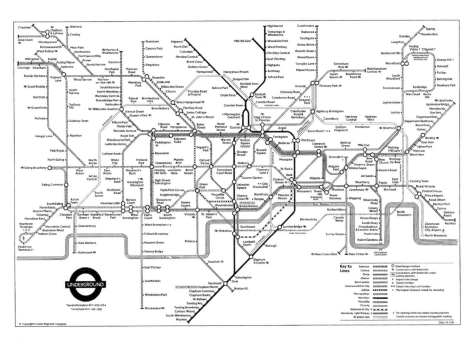

The London Underground (Registered Exempt User No. 99/E/969)

LT managers see their customers as not just comprising passengers on the transport system but Londoners in general. Hence, issues of a social benefit character are deemed to be of great importance. One of these benefits is to reduce road traffic and another to provide a serviceable system to the business community, enabling companies to develop new areas of business, etc.

LT managers estimate that the Underground system needs about £400m (at 1997 prices) per year for the improvement and refurbishment of the existing network and its infrastructure. According to press comment following the 1991 Monopolies and Mergers Commission report, this amount ought to be at least £700m per annum. Substantial additional funding has also been required for the construction of new lines, such as the Jubilee Line Extension (JLE). The view, held both publicly and by LT managers, is that the system has suffered years of neglect and underinvestment. Despite current levels of funding, for example, in 1991 the Government invested more than £1bn in LT, this view prevails and gained increased public attention during the London mayor election campaign in 2000.

Table 3.4 Capital expenditure, LT	
Underground (core, excluding Jubilee Line Extension)	£374m
Underground (Jubilee Line Extension)	£660m
Buses (infrastructure)	£ 13m
Other	£ 11m
Total	£1,058m
The funding was obtained via:	£137m (internal)
	£921m (Government grants)
Source: 1996/97 LT Accounts	

Table 3.4 illustrates the capital spending by LT during 1996/97 and illustrates that the investment expenditure was dominated by the Jubilee Line Extension and that almost £400m that year was required to renew and replace Underground and bus assets owned by LT.

LT decision-making process

Because of limited funding, managers are constrained in the range of projects they can undertake. As a result, they have adopted a fairly sophisticated procedure of evaluating projects, which involves comparing benefits with costs. The principal factors which are considered in the appraisal procedure are those which relate to social benefits. Social benefits are generally held to be those affecting the community at large. A great deal of research has been conducted over some 30 years in how to measure these. The principal finding of these studies is the key concept that time is worth money. Hence, saving time represents a saving to customers. Accordingly, in the project appraisal procedure, the principal criterion used is the value passengers put on their time in their use of the Underground system. In other words, would the customer be prepared to pay more for a faster Underground service, for example, when compared with driving or using other means of transport? In particular, the research found that, in general, customers value their time spent on an underground journey to be worth about £5 an hour or 9p a minute at 1996/7 prices. In other words, they would be willing to pay 9p towards a time-saving project for every minute saved in journey time.

However, in addition to the time issue, there is a range of other factors which have a value or cost to customers. These factors are given a value which is incorporated in any capital budgeting process. These other factors associated with an Underground journey are considered to be 'softer' elements and are seen to improve journey features and also to possess a value to passengers. These items are listed below, not necessarily in order of importance.

- Quality of travel information communicated to passengers
- Cleanliness of stations and trains
- How secure users of the network feel

Negative factors include:

- Waiting, climbing stairs, 'hassle' factors, congestion (the latter are given high values).
- Time spent queuing for tickets.

Consider safety benefits. What are the costs of risk to life? It is difficult to attribute a value to safety improvements. It is also very difficult to quantify pollution, although recent government research findings have been able to put costs on certain types of pollution, specifically their effect on health treatment costs.

As we have already shown, behavioural research by LT has attached values to time and to other factors. These values were derived from so-called *real preference* techniques and are as accurate as can be estimated. The findings of the research suggest that designated values can be attributed to each factor and to trade-offs. Alternative sets of scenarios can be calculated, such as 'high fare short journey time', 'long journey lower fare'. LT estimated that customers were willing to pay 6p per journey for perfect cleanliness and feeling safe, 7p per journey for perfect travel information, etc. at 1996/7 prices.

Additional cost factors to be considered in the pricing process are:

- The trade-off between crowded and empty trains. What are the implied values to be considered? For example, is a customer happy to wait five minutes for another train in order to get a seat?
- Are passengers able to take lifts/escalators or must they walk downstairs? What value do people put on this alternative?

A typical underground journey can be valued on the basis of the notion 'what it feels like to you'. For a trip of about 25 minutes, which is the average journey time, the actual fare is about 110p (1996/7 prices), the value of sitting/standing on the train is about 120p, waiting time 50p and so on. This produces a 'what it feels like' value of about £3.50.

The final outcome of the costing exercise must culminate in which value factors provided to passengers result in a general acceptance of the journeys' fares. For example, the total sum ought to include 'pain' factors (such as waiting, long walks, congestion).

The ultimate question, which LT managers, working for a publicly owned organisation, must consider, is whether they can raise fares and thus increase revenues. The increases could, for example, be justified by providing quicker journey times, improved quality, etc. A private-sector organisation would probably be less encumbered by the social responsibilities LT managers feel they must respond to, and most probably could increase Underground fare prices more readily. The dilemma that LT managers face is therefore whether to reduce fares or increase levels of service. The principal rule, which managers claim to follow, is that LT should always examine all factors and review how the circumstances affect the customers' 'feel like' values.

In response to research, some of the positive value factors have been identified as priorities by LT and integrated into management targets, such as public address systems on platforms and in trains.

In addition to the above costing analysis, LT examines the external benefits and external costs of specific elements of a project. These externalities will not appear in LT's financial accounts but may well affect other people or organisations financially or in other ways. For example, external benefits may include a reduction in congestion or accident prevention; external costs may include noise pollution from new trains. LT quantifies these externalities for large projects, such as the JLE, main line extensions, and station upgrades and renewal projects.

The JLE project was an extremely large infrastructure investment, finally approved by the UK government in 1993 after years of lobbying and evaluation. The main intention was to develop the transport facilities to the eastern part of London and particularly to the redeveloped Docklands area. This redevelopment was designed to attract commercial organisations as well as to enhance residential facilities. A new and efficient Underground line, which connected to the existing network, was seen to be the vital element in the development plans.

Because of the magnitude of the JLE project, and the wide range of implications of such a project, the appraisal factors incorporated issues which are not normally considered in LT's conventional investment programme. The major elements which were considered in the investment appraisal for the JLE were:

- *regionalisation benefits* – How would a new line improve an area of London?

- *transportation benefits* – What were the demographic advantages of a new line?

- *wider economic benefits* – What extra income would the new line generate for the communities along its route?

In Paris the same methodology is used for the Métro network, but not for the larger rail network.

In the JLE project appraisal, broader benefits to society, such as an increase in general investment near the new stations, improved labour skills, etc., were also examined. The investment appraisal procedure included an analysis which compared economic activity with the existence of a new underground line and with no underground development at all.

Funding issues

LT is able to use revenues generated by its operations for the funding of capital projects (refer back to Table 3.4 for a funding breakdown). The table shows that government provides the bulk of project capital as LT is (a) unable to generate sufficient cash flows from its operations for the necessary projects and (b) cannot raise funds in external capital markets (limits are predetermined under the 1984 Act) other than through the Private Finance Initiative (PFI), described in more detail in Section 5.2 of this unit.

Refer to Unit 1 for a discussion of real and nominal discount rates.

LT applies a 6% *real* discount rate to capital appraisals and this rate is the real rate of return (ROR) required by government and determined by HM Treasury. In essence, investment in a public-sector project can proceed as long as it meets the ROR (6% real rate). The 6% real rate represents the hurdle rate for public-sector projects and is designed to exceed the cost of capital to government. However, the level of risk of particular projects may require adjustment to the ROR. If a public-sector project is financed privately, it is the private sector's ROR which becomes relevant and the transfer of risk to the private sector also becomes crucial.

This is discussed in more detail in Section 5, Funding Capital Projects.

LT managers acknowledge that their appraisal procedure is unable to evaluate all the risk factors which exist in any capital project. The rules state that in projects which are funded through the PFI route, LT must diversify away as many risks as practicable. As a result, specific project risks have to be quantified in the appraisal process. Although the number of PFI-funded projects in LT has been limited, the public/private partnership approach to funding public-sector projects is being adopted in a number of countries. The issue of risk transfer between the public and private sectors has acquired a pivotal role in such projects.

3.4 INFLATION AND TAXATION

The discussion in Section 3.2 on the issues in appraisal techniques ignored inflation and taxation. These two subjects are important and, as a result, we devote a separate section to them. Inflation and taxation have a major impact on CAPEX investment appraisals, in that they are able to significantly influence project cash-flow profiles.

Inflation

The correct treatment of inflation requires that we compare like with like in the financial appraisal. This means that real cash flows should be discounted at a real discount rate or nominal cash flows discounted at a nominal rate. There is clearly potential for a mismatch of assumptions regarding cash flows and discount rates. The most obvious pitfall is to use a nominal discount rate derived from financial market data and apply this to current price or real cash flows. This would result in NPV values being understated. In some cases this could contribute to the rejection of project proposals. The converse situation can also occur where nominal cash flows are discounted at the real discount rate. This mismatch will result in NPV calculations being overestimated.

Even if the cash flows and discount rates are correctly specified (both in real terms or both in nominal terms), cash flow and discount rate estimates must include a consistent estimate of expected inflation. Any mismatch of inflation assumptions embedded in cash flows and in the discount rate can have a pronounced effect on longer-term projects because the effects of the failure to allow for inflation in cash-flow estimates compound with time. Under these circumstances distant cash flows have present values which may be seriously distorted compared with nearer ones. Such possibility for error may explain the preference in many organisations for shorter-term projects and the use of payback.

Exercise 3.1 _____

Suppose you are forecasting a project which will generate sales growing at around 5% per year for ten years. The discount rate you have been asked to use is based on a risk-free rate from a quoted 10-year government bond of 10%. You are also aware that 10-year index-linked government bonds have a *real* yield of 3%. What is the implied *real* growth rate in sales?

Taxation

Although Section 4.4.3 of *Vital Statistics* explains the mathematical treatment of taxation in the capital budgeting appraisal procedure, some additional comments may help you to understand this important topic.

The main point that we stress in this unit, and indeed in the whole of this course, is that if an organisation can produce high cash flows for its stakeholders it is valuable. Since taxes typically represent a large cash flow that goes to one stakeholder (the tax collector) at the expense of others, it is important for financial managers, and in effect all managers, to understand the basics of the taxation system, for the following reasons.

- Virtually every financial decision changes the amount of taxes the organisation or its stakeholders will pay. It is impossible to evaluate a decision in financial terms without including the impact of taxes.

- If there are more ways than one to accomplish a goal, and if they differ in their tax impact, the amount of the tax cash flows must enter the decision-making process for the comparison to be complete.

- Tax authorities require only what is specified by law, and the organisation fully satisfies its tax obligations by paying the specified amount. An organisation that pays more tax than it needs is taking value away from the other stakeholders.

Section 4.2 of Unit 4 introduced the issue of taxation in the context of the capital structure of the firm. The text notes that debt financing is cheaper, after tax, than equity. This concept can be carried forward into the context of capital investment funding.

Taxation can have an important influence on the capital investment decision, in that there exists a fundamental difference between debt and equity funding. If, for example, a capital project is funded by equity capital, no tax benefits will accrue, whereas interest on debt-funded investments is tax deductible. In many countries interest payments on debt are allowable for taxation, which means that the taxation liability is reduced. In one sense, the impact of the tax deductibility of interest expense is to create an asset, normally referred to as the 'tax shield', because the expected future post-tax cash flows are increased. As with all assets, it is possible to derive a value for this debt-created tax shield by calculating the present value of its expected future cash flows. The expected future cash flows can be estimated by computing the expected reduction in future tax payments caused by the required

Refer to Unit 4.

interest payments on the debt financing. Alternatively, if the tax rate and debt/equity ratio are assumed constant throughout the life of the project, as was the case in Unit 4, the value of the tax shield can be included through the factor $(1 - T)$ in the WACC formula.

The issues described in the previous paragraph are liable to cause some controversy when the hurdle rate for a particular project is to be determined. Should the firm use the *average* cost of capital for the firm, the WACC, or the *marginal* cost of capital for the project in question?

Capital allowances is the UK term for tax-deductible depreciation allowances.

It should be noted that tax deductible or **capital allowances** and changes in tax rates affect after-tax cash flows. Capital allowances, although not cash flows, provide a tax shield for revenues. In order to improve the realism of investment appraisals, DCF methods should use after-tax cash flows in the assessment of project proposals. However, the tax rates and allowable depreciation rates valid when analysing an investment may not be the ones in effect when the project is implemented. Any such changes can cause the actual NPV and IRR amounts to differ significantly from those originally estimated for the project.

Finally, you may now be under the impression that tax must be considered in every project appraisal. Note, however, that many organisations are not legally required to pay tax, including charities and many public sector organisations. Nevertheless, these types of organisations spend funds on capital projects. In addition, loss-making companies do not pay tax either. However, their circumstances are different again, in that losses can be carried forward under the assumption that eventually the company will become profitable again.

Activity 3.3 _____

Discuss what in your opinion is the impact of taxation on the Channel Tunnel project.

Because the Channel Tunnel is a project of a long-term nature it will be subject to a range of changing tax factors over time. In the early years it has been loss-making, building up tax losses against which future profits may be offsettable. In time, economic activity will increase and profit will be made but this will generate an increased tax burden. Taxation rates may change over time, which could alter the profile of the tax payments. All these factors will impact upon the taxation charges and, in addition, managers will be able to make decisions which will affect the tax flows.

3.5 INTERNATIONAL CAPITAL BUDGETING

No discussion about capital budgeting is complete without considering it in an international context. In the same way as for domestic capital investment decisions, international capital budgeting focuses on expected incremental cash flows linked to the project. The same difficulties apply to assessing these cash flows but international project appraisal is often more complex, in that, for example, a multinational company must consider factors specific to the international environment, as well as financial issues such as cross-border taxation and foreign currency risk.

Complexities in international capital investment projects often arise because foreign projects can have sizeable consequences on other divisions of the group. For example, a multinational engineering group, intending to build a facility in Spain, may discover that the proposed project will affect the operations of other parts of the company. The sales of products of the new facility may affect the sales of divisions in the Netherlands and Denmark. Where such events occur, the organisation needs to appraise the project by combining all incremental cash flows. Thus, while the cash flows in Spain are clearly relevant, so are the reduced cash flows to the Dutch and Danish divisions.

Additional complexities inherent in international capital budgeting can be divided into micro and macro factors (Buckley, 1998).

For example, micro factors include the following:

- differing project and parent cash flows (due to difficulties in remitting cash to the parent)
- part of the parent input may be of a non-cash-flow nature, e.g. through provision of equipment
- royalties and management fees may be involved

Macro factors include:

- exchange rates may not be constant throughout the project's life
- exchange rate movements do not reflect purchasing power parity (see Unit 8)
- different tax rates may apply in the host country and the parent's country

A project may generate substantial cash flows abroad, but because of exchange control restrictions, it may be impossible to repatriate some or all of these foreign cash flows back to the parent company. If you appraise a foreign project under these conditions, the potential project cash flows may still encourage investment. However, is this good enough? It is generally accepted that the present value of a project is a function of future cash flows distributable to the investors or owners. But if the greater part of the foreign cash flows were blocked by exchange controls, only the residual cash flows could be transmitted back to the parent company. Which cash flows should be considered?

International capital projects can be viewed from two standpoints – incremental project cash flows or incremental parent cash flows. First, project cash flows can be determined from the foreign division's standpoint, as if it were an independent entity, and solely analysed from within the host country. The second stage moves to the parent company and focuses on the amount and timing of distributable cash flows. This analysis should also take account of the taxes payable in the various countries, of which more later in this section.

Block 4 will deal with the topics of foreign exchange and interest rates.

If no exchange controls exist in the host country, all foreign project cash flows should be repatriable, although changes in exchange rates and taxation issues must be taken into account. If exchange controls are in place, further complexities are added to the decision-making process. There are ways by which remittances to the parent can be achieved despite exchange controls. For example:

- Repatriating dividends from abroad to host country
- Payment of royalties and management fees
- Loan repayments
- Countertrade.

(Buckley, 1998)

Countertrade involves a reciprocal agreement for the exchange of goods or services. The parties involved may be companies or governments, and these agreements can take a number of forms, for example, barter, counter purchase, industrial offset (reciprocal arrangements to buy materials or components from sources in the foreign country). Such methods to avoid unremittable profits may change the project from being undesirable to acceptable.

Finally, although international taxation is a complex subject, we must devote a few paragraphs to this topic.

We have discussed international capital budgeting from the standpoint of the parent company. Any project cash flows will in the first place be subject to host country taxes. Then, upon distribution (or presumed distribution) to the parent, the cash flows may be subject to a **withholding tax** (a tax levied on dividends paid abroad which are expatriated to another country) and finally to corporation tax of the parent's home country.

Let us provide an example which illustrates this procedure. Assume that a firm with a proposed project abroad has provided an earnings forecast equivalent to £1m in pre-tax profit. With a tax rate in the host country of 15%, a withholding tax rate of 10% and a home country corporation tax rate of 33%, we show the numbers to be incorporated in the investment appraisal in Table 3.5.

Table 3.5 Project appraisal – parent company cash flows net of taxes		
	£	£
Profit generated before tax		1,000,000
Foreign tax charge, @15%	(150,000)	
Withholding tax charge £1m × 85% (foreign post-tax profit) = £850,000 @ 10%	(85,000)	
		(235,000)
Home country tax		
£1m @ 33%	(330,000)	
Foreign tax credit	235,000	
		(95,000)
Providing net of tax home country profit		670,000

NB: Foreign tax credit is the amount of tax paid in a foreign country claimed by the company as a credit against home country tax.

Please note that in Table 3.5 we have ignored any potential capital allowances which might accrue to the firm.

We assume that the above investment scenario takes place under a tax regime in which all foreign taxes paid are credited against home country tax liabilities. This may not always be the case and will depend on the particular tax treaty in operation between the two countries concerned. If full double tax relief were not available, for example, the project proposal might not generate a positive NPV for the parent company. However, the project might look acceptable by, for example, rerouting funds around the world without being returned to the home country, thus avoiding the 33% tax charge. Relevant tax information such as this ought to be included in the decision-making process and will enhance managers' ability to make optimal international investment decisions.

One could infer from the above scenario, which exemplifies a heavy tax regime as well as difficulties in the repatriation of profits to the home country, that many countries discourage direct foreign investment. On the contrary, many countries are now competing with each other to attract multinational organisations and investments. These countries offer a range of incentives which include:

- low corporate taxation rates (Isle of Man)
- tax relief on a range of inward investments (UK)
- subsidies (regional grants and European Union grants)
- taxation holidays (i.e. firms can operate for five years in the guest country without paying taxes, e.g. Ireland).

Essentially, two major factors for multinationals deciding whether or not to invest in a country/location are the tax regulations and incentives.

Finally, there is evidence that multinational organisations charge all of their foreign projects (for investment appraisal purposes) with a hypothetical average home tax rate that smoothes out anomalies (Buckley, 1998). Perhaps the best appraisal approach for projects abroad is to apply the harshest tax treatment to a base case and then apply sensitivity analysis assuming either zero home country tax or the average home country tax rate. This type of exercise would provide additional data to decision-makers in their continual quest for 'perfect' capital appraisal techniques.

International capital budgeting is also an issue for governmental organisations. Most developed countries provide foreign aid to less developed countries, often in the form of aid projects in which expertise and fixed assets are supplied from the donor country to the recipient country. These projects are weighed up in part on the basis of the benefits to the recipient country and of the costs of the donor country. No doubt, also, matters of international politics and diplomacy play a part. One issue they raise is how and how much donor country taxpayers benefit from projects and services provided in host countries.

SUMMARY

In this section we discussed a range of inter-related issues on the subject of investment appraisal techniques. We studied a range of appraisal techniques used by organisations. Not only must we understand the use of the correct appraisal techniques, but also the overall context of the CAPEX decision process in which the choice of technique takes place.

The article you were asked to read as Activity 3.1 provides some insights on how the decision-making process is conducted in practice. In some organisations managers manipulate the process in order to advance their own project proposals in a financially constrained environment.

The study of London Transport provided a picture of the difficulties and complex issues in CAPEX decisions which management face in order to provide passengers with expected levels of service.

Inflation and taxation add to the complexity of project evaluation and they were briefly discussed in the context of CAPEX. Under conditions of inflation, cash flows and discount rates are difficult to estimate. We also examined aspects of taxation in the context of CAPEX appraisals and the potential effect tax has on the cash flow profiles over the life of a project.

Finally, as many organisations operate in an international environment, it is important to review aspects of international capital budgeting, since managers have an additional range of complicating factors in their decision-making process. At the same time, taxation is an important consideration for multinational organisations in their foreign investment programmes.

4 RISK ISSUES IN CAPEX

We consider financial risk in various guises throughout this course, such as in Unit 1(Sections 2 and 3), which explains how to measure risk relative to return; and Unit 4, which views risk from a capital structure viewpoint. In addition, the whole of Block 4 will be concerned with financial risk and the methods used by organisations to manage and minimise it. In this section, we focus on risk in the context of capital project investment. It is important to recognise, and learn how to deal with, the specific types of risk issues which relate to CAPEX, because they are intrinsically intertwined with investment decision-making processes. We describe a number of methods which can measure risk, such as simple risk-adjustment and probabilistic risk analysis.

In this section, we also describe some recent trends and developments in the field of project appraisal. There is a consensus that the DCF model is deficient for solving the arithmetic of certain kinds of investment decisions. The hypothesis we present is that the traditional DCF and other appraisal rules may be adequate to appraise pure cash-saving investment projects but leave something to be desired where there is a requirement for operational flexibility, or contingent opportunities for growth. In these circumstances a capital project may be considered an option to invest. We suggest that DCF methods consistently undervalue projects due to their failure to allow for strategic flexibility (Buckley, 1998). This compels managers to focus their thinking and practice in a direction where the choice of capital investment alternatives must be considered in a wider context. In the public sector, with subjectivity and wider cost/benefit issues and externalities, these broader considerations are more common. Ironically, in recent years, the public sector has been under pressure to act along stricter economic lines, encouraging a narrower view of the worth of investment projects.

4.1 HOW TO DEAL WITH RISK?

In the organisational context we must assume that managers are risk-averse, or at the very least want to minimise planning and operating risks.

A substantive element of the capital budgeting process is concerned with the selection of an appropriate discount factor. The correct discount rate is simply the opportunity cost of capital for a particular project, that is the expected rate of return that could be earned from an investment of similar risk. In theory the opportunity cost should reflect the non-diversifiable, or *systematic,* risk that is associated with a particular project, as outlined in the capital asset pricing model (CAPM). This risk might have characteristics that differ from those of the organisation's other individual projects or from its average investment programme. In practice, however, the opportunity cost of a particular project may be difficult to determine and, as we saw in Unit 4, many organisations use the weighted average cost of capital (WACC) as a substitute. The WACC offers a good approximation as long as the organisation's projects do not differ from one another in their non-diversifiable risks and as long as this risk is likely to stay constant for the life of the projects.

Refer to Unit 4 and *Vital Statistics* (Section 5.2.5) for descriptions of the CAPM.

The CAPM was developed in the context of financial investment. Since its development, academics and practitioners have struggled with the task of extending and applying the framework to capital investment, with only limited success. At the same time, in the volatile commercial environment, the problem of handling risk has grown. Uncertainty in the underlying economic environment has increased because of the considerable instabilities in future inflation levels, tax rates and exchange rates.

Project risk usually indicates that the results of an investment decision are inherently imprecise and consequently may have undesirable outcomes or losses. An integrative model for handling project risk was developed by Ho and Pike (1991) who suggested that all investment decisions in practice should go through a series of steps in a logical manner. This requires:

(i) risk identification

(ii) application of methods of reducing the risk

(iii) risk evaluation and its subsequent incorporation in the financial project appraisal.

Attempts by organisations to reflect the differential risks inherent in projects fall into two broadly identifiable categories:

(i) Simple risk adjustment methods based on deterministic estimations and intuitive adjustments to either the underlying cash flows or the economic evaluation model (e.g. changing the discount factor or the payback criterion for projects carrying different levels of risk).

(ii) **Probabilistic risk analysis** (**PRA**) techniques based on the evaluation of the uncertainties associated with critical variables and their probabilities before any risk–return trade-off is made. Commonly used PRA techniques include **sensitivity analysis**, **probability analysis**, **decision tree analysis** and **Monte Carlo simulation**.

You will be asked to read a version of the Ho and Pike survey in Unit 7 which looks at risk management techniques. In this unit we look briefly at the types of technique used by managers in practice.

From both a theoretical and an intuitive perspective, investors taking a greater risk should be compensated with greater expected returns. This applies to investment in capital assets as well as investment in financial assets. In a survey (Ho and Pike, 1991) a number of organisations were asked to rank in order of importance the use of risk assessment techniques for projects of higher perceived risk than that of the company as a whole, and they are in descending order of frequency:

- applying sensitivity analysis, combined with the best/worst case analysis

- shortening the required payback period

- raising the discount rate/required rate of return

- using probability analysis

- adjusting estimated cash flows subjectively

- adjusting estimated cash flows for cost of risk premium

- using **certainty equivalent** cash flows. Certainty equivalents are attained by replacing each period's expected cash flow by the 'certain' cash flow that would be equivalent in value or utility (a rather cumbersome method).

Table 4.1 shows the level of use by organisations of the above techniques in capital investment appraisal processes. The objective of the survey was to examine UK managers' attitudes towards, and practices of, risk analysis. Although the survey was published in 1991 (the most recent survey available), there is no evidence that the usage trends of the various adjustment methods for risk have changed dramatically. However, the increasingly widespread use of personal computers with financial modelling packages has added to the potential, ease of use and efficiency of risk analysis in capital budgeting.

The Ho and Pike survey showed, for example, that the use of probability analysis is limited to a small percentage of organisations on a regular basis. Nevertheless, managers who use probability analysis take the view that the information required for such an analysis offers valuable insights and increases the level of confidence in the final decision.

Very few organisations use one technique exclusively. The use of two or more risk-adjusting techniques is common, and many organisations use four or more methods. The most popular combinations of risk adjustments are raised discount rate/required rate of return *and* shortened required payback period; and raised discount rate/required rate of return *and* shortened required payback period *and* subjective adjustment of estimated cash flow. This may indicate that there is deemed to be no single method for management to determine an acceptable level of project risk.

Table 4.1 Risk appraisal techniques								
	Mostly frequently		$\rightarrow$		**Least frequently**			
Risk Adjustment Method Used	**1**	**2**	**3**	**4**	**5**	**Total used**	**Not used**	**Exclusive use**
	%	%	%	%	%	%	%	%
1. Raise discount rate/ required rate of return	42.1	23.2	9.8	6.8	2.3	84.2	15.8	6.76
2. Shorten required payback period	33.8	25.6	14.5	5.3	3.8	83.0	17.0	3.00
3. Adjust estimated cash flows subjectively/ intuitively	22.6	17.3	15.8	7.5	6.0	69.2	30.8	4.51
4. Use expected values or certainty equivalent of cash flows*	15.0	8.3	9.8	11.3	12.1	56.4	43.6	2.25
5. Adjust estimated cash flows for costs of risk premium	1.5	3.0	9.8	12.8	23.3	50.4	49.6	0.00

Note: 13 respondents did not indicate any adjustments. The percentages in this Table are based on 133 firms that stated they did adjust for risk, not on the total number of firms in the survey.

* These two techniques are not the same. 'Expected values' is based on probabilities, and 'certainty equivalents' on utility theory using risk/return trade-off. They are grouped together here to facilitate comparison with previous findings with similar categorisation.

Source: Ho and Pike (1991)

A minority of the firms reviewed by Ho and Pike used the CAPM to determine the required discount rate. For those companies which used the CAPM to assist in determining the overall cost of capital, few used it specifically to adjust for project risk. The general consensus appears to be that the extent of the discount rate adjustment for a particular project should be a matter of managerial judgement.

At this point let us go back to the use of NPV in the context of attributing risk to a capital investment project proposal. In an uncertain world, even assuming perfect capital markets, all that the NPV method can do is to evaluate the *expected* cash flows of a project.

When examining the rationale behind the NPV method, managers often pay little attention to how the estimates of the future cash flows are derived. In practice, managers are unlikely to produce a series of single-figure estimates of each year's cash flows, but usually attempt to establish a range of estimates. For example, they may estimate the annual cash flows based on three economic states: boom, normal and recession conditions. From these data the project's NPV may be calculated for each state and the probability or likelihood of each state actually occurring may be applied. The **expected net present value (ENPV)** of the project is based on the different estimates and their probabilities of occurrence. It is on the magnitude of the ENPV that an investment appraisal decision may be determined.

BOX 4.1 PARAISO PLC

In this example, the ENPV of a project is estimated for Paraiso plc.

Paraiso plc is considering whether to purchase a machine to produce glue for ceramic tiles. The machine costs £1,000 and is expected to have a productive life of three years. However, the estimate of the annual net revenue from the machine is uncertain and depends on the state of the house-building industry. The company's management have produced the following estimates:

	State of Industry	0 (£)	1 (£)	2 (£)	3 (£)
				Year	
(i)	Boom	−1,000	+500	+700	+980
(ii)	Normal	−1,000	+500	+600	+700
(iii)	Depressed	−1,000	+300	+300	+250

Paraiso normally use a 10% discount rate in project appraisal, believing that this currently reflects the risk of the project. On this basis, the project NPVs have been calculated as follows:

State	NPV (£)
(i)	+769.4
(ii)	+476.3
(iii)	−291.5

Latest figures from the Building Trades Research Institute suggest the following probabilities for the industry's future prospects:

State	Probability
Boom	0.20
Normal	0.60
Depressed	0.20

On this basis, Paraiso plc estimate the project's expected (i.e. arithmetic mean) NPV:

State	Probability		NPV (£)		(£)
(i)	0.20	×	+769.4	=	+153.9
(ii)	0.60	×	+476.3	=	+285.8
(iii)	0.20	×	−291.5	=	−58.3
				ENPV	+381.4

As the project has a positive expected net present value (ENPV), it is accepted.

Exercise 4.1

Rework the numbers with the probabilities of the economic states being 0.1 for boom, 0.3 for normal and 0.6 for depressed. Does the final ENPV of the project still warrant consideration of the proposal?

Managers find ENPV useful because it provides an average value of the proposed project's performance. However, you must be aware that ENPV does not take account of risk, because all that ENPV analysis shows is a measure of the investment's *expected* results, whereas risk is concerned with the likelihood that the *actual* results may differ from what is expected.

Risk-averse managers, investing in capital projects of any kind, may be more concerned that an investment may perform below expectations, that is, with 'downside' risk rather than its 'upside' potential. In this case, what managers are actually doing is looking at one side of the probability distribution more than the other.

Instead of being sophisticated about the probability distributions of project outcomes, most organisations prefer to use relatively simple risk adjustment techniques such as a risk-adjusted discount rate or even a standard WACC, and *then* apply sensitivity analysis. This typical method of managing risk involves the choice of a discount factor to allow for *systematic* risk (as, for example, in the CAPM) and the application of a payback criterion which allows (in an approximate way) for *total* risk. In addition, managers employ their judgement based on experience and knowledge of their business to allow for any unacceptable downside risk or as yet unquantifiable upside potential. However, a significant number of financiers and managers use a comprehensive risk checklist in their evaluation of the impact of each risk on a proposed project's NPV (Nevitt, 1989).

4.2 INVESTMENT PROJECTS AS OPTIONS

The economic environment in which most companies must now operate is volatile and unpredictable, due to moves towards globalisation of markets, increases in exchange rate fluctuations and rapid technology-induced changes in the market-place. Whatever its cause, however, uncertainty requires that managers become much more sophisticated in the ways they assess and account for risk. It is important for managers to get a better understanding of the options that their companies have or that they are able to create. Ultimately, options create flexibility, and, in an uncertain world, the ability to value and use flexibility is critical.

What this means is that managers must not solely rely on the NPV rule in CAPEX decision-making. To make intelligent investment choices managers need to consider the value of keeping their options open, as W.H. Smith did by taking the Lakeside site, although a conventional NPV appraisal, in which competitor exclusion was not considered, might have suggested otherwise.

At this stage we must briefly introduce the concept of options (which will be dealt with in greater depth in Unit 9). If we note that opportunities are options, i.e. rights but not obligations to take some action in the future, then capital investments are essentially about options. An organisation with an opportunity to invest in a capital project is in fact holding a **financial call option**. It has the right but not the obligation to make an investment outlay in a project (in return for the entitlement to a stream of profits/cash flows from the project) at a future time of its choosing. When a company makes the investment outlay, it 'exercises' in effect its call option.

The purpose of this section is to examine the shortcomings of the conventional approaches to CAPEX decision-making and to present a different approach for thinking about investment procedures. The standard NPV method of appraising capital project proposals suggests that managers should:

(i)   determine an appropriate discount rate

(ii) calculate the PV of the stream of expenditures incurred when undertaking the project

(iii) calculate the PV of the expected stream of cash flows that the investment will generate, and

(iv) determine the difference between the two – the NPV of the project.

If the NPV is greater than zero, applying the NPV decision rule suggests that management should go ahead with the investment.

It would be naïve to believe, however, that the NPV rule is applied without recourse to other considerations. In practice, managers often seek a consensus projection for the cash flow streams or, as we have seen with ENPV, use an average of high, medium and low estimates. However, managers are often unaware of making an implicit faulty assumption, which is that the implementation or development of a project begins at a fixed point in time, usually the present. In effect, the NPV rule assumes a fixed scenario in which an investment is made which, when completed, generates cash flows during its expected life cycle, without any contingencies. More importantly, although the NPV rule requires managers to consider all relevant cash flows, even if not directly related to the particular project, it does not suggest that managers explore the impact of delaying the project or abandoning it if market conditions change adversely. Instead, the NPV rule compares investing today with *never* investing. A more useful technique would be to examine a range of possibilities: investing today, or waiting one or two years, etc.

Unfortunately, the basic NPV rule, although relatively easy to apply, is built on a restrictive assumption. It assumes that a project must be started immediately – a 'now or never' proposition – and cannot be delayed. Although some investment decisions fall into the above category, most do not. It is often possible to delay investment decisions. This possibility of delay can be valuable as, for example, in the case of an oil exploration company which delays drilling for oil until the results of geological surveys have been analysed or of a pharmaceutical company which wants to delay investment in a production line for a new drug until it has obtained approval to sell the drug in the USA.

However, once undertaken, such investment may be irreversible, in the sense that once the project is started, it cannot be 'reversed' at no cost. If it could be, there would be no value in being able to delay the project.

So how does a company choose when to exercise that option? In exercising its option by making an irreversible investment, the organisation effectively 'kills' the option. This means that, by deciding to invest, the organisation forgoes the possibility of waiting for new information that might affect the desirability or timing of the project; it cannot disinvest should market conditions change adversely. The lost option value is an opportunity cost that must be included as part of the cost of investing *now*. As a result the simple NPV rule must be modified. Instead of being greater than or equal to zero, the PV of the expected cash flow streams must exceed the cost of the project by an amount equal to the value of keeping the investment option alive.

This opportunity cost is highly sensitive to uncertainty over the future value of the project. New economic conditions may affect the perceived riskiness of future cash flows and have a large impact on investment spending (larger, for example, than the impact of a change in interest rates and hence discount rates). Viewing capital investments as options puts greater emphasis on the role of risk and less emphasis on interest rates and other variables.

The recognition that CAPEX decisions can be irreversible adds significance to the ability to delay investments. In reality, organisations do not always have the opportunity to delay investing in capital projects. For example, strategic considerations can make it imperative for a company to invest quickly in order to pre-empt investment by a competitor. In most cases however, it is at least feasible to delay. There may be a cost – the risk of entry by rivals or the loss of cash flows – but the cost can be set off against the benefits of waiting for new information, and those benefits are often substantial.

We have suggested that an irreversible investment opportunity is like a financial call option (see Unit 9). The holder of the call option has the right, for a specified period, to pay an exercise price and to receive in return an asset which has some value. Exercising the option is irreversible, one cannot retrieve the option or the funding that was paid to exercise it. Similarly, an organisation with an investment opportunity has the option to expend funds (the 'exercise price') now or in the future in return for an asset of some value (the project). The asset or project can be sold to another company, but the investment itself is irreversible. As with a financial call option, the option to undertake a CAPEX is valuable in part because the future value of the asset obtained by investing is uncertain. If the asset increases in value, the net benefit from investing increases. On the other hand, if the value declines, the organisation can decide not to invest and will lose only what it has spent to obtain the investment opportunity. As long as there are some conditions under which the organisation would prefer not to invest (when there is some probability that the project would result in a loss), the opportunity to delay the decision, and thus keep its option open, has value. So, given that the option exists, the question then arises as to when to exercise it. The choice of the most appropriate time is the essence of the optimal investment decision.

If management can recognise that an investment opportunity is like a financial call option it can help them to understand the crucial role uncertainty plays in the timing of CAPEX decisions.

However, it is important to appreciate that the options approach to CAPEX decisions is *very* difficult to apply to most types of industries or services. The use of options is considered to be most appropriate to R&D, mineral and natural resource projects.

Finally, the economic environment in which organisations must function is volatile. These variable conditions require sophisticated methods of risk management. Management need to understand the options that their organisations have or are able to create. Ultimately, options create flexibility, and, in an uncertain world, the ability to value and use flexibility is critical. This means that simply applying the NPV rule to the CAPEX appraisals is not sufficient. Management must be able to make intelligent investment decisions and be able to consider constantly the value of keeping their options open.

Although the above appears to constitute a fairly strong indictment of the classical DCF approach to CAPEX processes, it would be wrong to state, however, that the DCF approach is without merit, or that it should be discarded in favour of a simpler method, such as the payback rule.

Activity 4.2

Read the article by Dixit and Pindyck entitled 'The options approach to capital investment' in the Course Reader. This article explains the options approach to capital investment in a non-mathematical way and gives a number of real-world examples. If you have time, read the Course Reader article by Leslie and Michaels entitled 'Real options'. This looks at how option theory was applied to project investment for BP and National Power.

SUMMARY

In this section, we examined the issues surrounding risk in relation to CAPEX. We explained a number of methods which can measure risk, such as simple risk-adjustment and probabilistic risk analysis. We also provided information as to what risk adjustment techniques organisations are using in their management of risk. We mentioned sensitivity analysis, shortened payback, discount rate adjustments, the adjustment of cash flows and the use of certainty equivalents.

We included an activity where you are asked to examine the expected net present value, which illustrates how to estimate project cash flows under a range of economic situations. This is achieved by applying probabilities to the range of cash flows which are estimated to be generated by the project under review.

We then examined the CAPEX decision-making process in the light of the ability to take out an option on a project proposal which could be exercised now or at a future date. We decided that since an option has value it should be taken into account when considering whether to invest in a project *now*. In particular, we noted that the option to delay or defer a project is more valuable the greater the uncertainty about future cash flows and the lower the initial project cash flows which would be lost or postponed by waiting. We stated that there are inherent problems with applying the traditional NPV rule to a range of investment decisions in that it ignores the option to delay investment.

5 FUNDING CAPITAL PROJECTS

So far, our discussion has been confined to an evaluation of capital investment appraisal, the effect of corporate strategy on the decision-making process and the problems of risk. We have not yet considered how capital projects should be funded, or whether one method of finance makes any difference compared with another method. In this section we describe various methods for funding of capital projects and the relative costs of these types of funding available to organisations of diverse characteristics.

Although earlier units in this course explain the issues dealing with raising capital, here we focus specifically on funding requirements for capital projects. This is in contrast to Unit 4 which considers finance tools and capital structure in general and Unit 6 in which the focus is on venture capital and merger and acquisition (M&A) funding activities.

We will first briefly revisit the equity- and debt-funding topics, although they have been described in some detail in Units 1 and 4. Leasing is an important method for financing plant and equipment and there are a number of advantages to using leasing over other funding methods. We will then look in more detail at project financing which is a method that has been used for many years to fund large, discrete projects.

Sections 5.2 and 5.3 consider the circumstances in which project finance is appropriate and provide a case study of how banks fund through project finance.

Finally, in Section 5.4, we shall look at the funding of public sector projects by private entities. In the UK, in recent years, this approach has gained favour in HM Treasury under such names as the Private Finance Initiative (PFI) and Public-Private Partnerships (PPPs).

5.1 EQUITY/DEBT FUNDING AND LEASING

In this section we discuss briefly some issues relating to the funding of CAPEX projects in the private sector.

Funds for capital investment generally tend to be from three (not necessarily mutually exclusive) sources: funding in the form of ordinary share capital or retained earnings, that is equity; funding in the form of interest-bearing medium- and long-term debt; and funding in the form of leasing. A capital project can be funded by a combination of equity, debt and leasing depending on a varied range of factors. Finally, there are other sources of long-term finance, such as government and EU grants.

The above three sources of finance vary in a number of ways. They differ in how they are raised, the obligations that they impose on the organisation's management, and how they are affected by taxation requirements. In addition, the differences of inherent risk of each method need careful examination. Unit 1, Section 2 showed that the return required on any investment should reflect the risk involved. Therefore, if these different types of finance have different levels of risk, you can expect their returns to reflect these differences.

Equity/debt funding

An essential feature of funding by shares or equity capital, which differs from most other forms of capital market finance, is that such funding rarely comes to maturity – the capital is permanent and need never be repaid. Shares can be sold to other investors thus transferring the permanent loan.

There are many forms of debt capital, but in general it can be defined as a loan made to an organisation which is normally repaid at some future date, although often debt is 'rolled over' by raising a loan to repay the earlier loan. Debt differs from equity in two fundamental ways:

(i) The providers of debt do not become owners of the firm but are merely creditors, since they are lending to the firm for a fixed period of time (there are rare exceptions to this practice). At the end of this final period the loan is repaid. In contrast, equity capital is permanent and never repaid except in such circumstances as liquidation.

Unit 2 also discusses the differences between debt and equity.

(ii) The suppliers of debt usually receive a contractually determined percentage return on their loan, known as the interest or **coupon rate**. This also contrasts with ordinary share capital, as the annual returns – dividends – are not obligatory and the level, if any are paid at all, is determined at the discretion of management.

Debt capital is ranked ahead of equity for the payment of annual returns. Legally, debt interest must be paid in full before any dividends are paid to shareholders. So, if there is a shortfall in the company's profits in a particular year, it is the ordinary shareholders who are more likely to suffer than the debt holders.

Given the contractual nature of the debt interest payments, the typically fixed term of the loan, and the fact that debt interest ranks before dividends, it is clear that debt is less risky than equity and hence the cost of debt is less than the cost of equity.

Leasing

Leasing is a form of secured borrowing specifically linked to CAPEX. Under a lease agreement, the owner of the asset, or **lessor**, leases (allows the use of) the asset to the **lessee** in return for agreed payments over a fixed term, exactly as in a debt agreement. However, since the lessor retains title to the asset, the loan is more secure than in the case of a conventional lender. Since it is less risky than ordinary lending, leasing can be an even cheaper form of finance than debt.

Over time, leasing has become an important source of finance for acquiring the use of assets, as an alternative to outright purchase. Leasing in the UK accounts for between 20% and 25% of all new assets acquired

(Samuels *et al.*, 1995). Leasing can therefore be seen as a source of finance and the 'lease or purchase' decision must be classed as a financing decision. In fact, leasing arrangements are economically *equivalent* to secured long-term debt. However, other writers maintain that the decision of whether to lease or not cannot be viewed as a pure financing decision, as it involves interactions with the investment decision (Lumby, 1995).

As the subject of leasing is a complex one and requires extensive examination, this section will concentrate on the principal issues. Leasing is a popular form of medium- or short-term finance. The distinguishing feature of a lease agreement is that one party (the lessee) obtains the use of an asset for a period of time, while the legal ownership of that asset remains with the other party (the lessor). A true leasing agreement, unlike a hire-purchase arrangement, does not give the lessee the right to final ownership.

Payments under a lease contract can vary in terms of time and amount and can be determined according to the lessee's requirements. When a lease is terminated, the leased equipment in law reverts to the lessor and thus any residual value of the underlying asset also belongs to the lessor. However, with long-term leasing agreements it is quite common for the lessee, when the period of the 'primary' lease has expired, to have the option to purchase the equipment for a nominal sum or to take out a 'secondary' lease. The latter means that the lessee can continue to use the facility, even though still not the legal owner. The rental payments during the period of the second lease are usually very low.

Leases can broadly be divided into two types of contracts, finance leases and operating leases. A **finance lease** usually means that the lessor is assured by the initial agreement of the full recovery of his or her financial outlay plus a suitable return on the capital invested. This type of lease is also known as a 'full payout' lease. The risks and rewards of ownership have effectively passed to the lessee. The risks and rewards from the use of the asset are, of course, also with the lessee. Undertaking a financial lease contract is the same as borrowing funds (Samuels *et al.*, 1995). The lessee undertakes a binding agreement to make the specified payments in the lease contract to the lessor. This is equivalent in cash-flow terms to borrowing the funds needed for the asset by entering into a binding contract to make interest and principal repayments to a lender.

An **operating lease** is usually for a shorter period than a finance lease. It is certainly for less than the estimated economic life of the asset. During the period of the lease contract the net cost of the asset to the lessor is not fully recovered. It is the lessor who retains the usual risks and rewards that come from the ownership of the equipment as distinct from the use of it. If the life of the asset turns out to be less than expected, due to obsolescence, it is the lessor who loses. As a result, the lessor normally assumes the responsibility for repairs, maintenance and insurance under an operating lease (in the case of aircraft, for example, or of property).

The life of an operating lease is not always known at the outset, for the lease may be cancelled or cover only a short period with options for continued short periods, each being less than the economic life of the asset. Where rental periods are extended, these will be on a negotiated economic basis. The rental payments, together with the tax and any other benefits received by the lessor over the period of a particular lease, will not necessarily cover the cost of the asset. The lessor may sell the asset at the end of any of the short periods of the lease. When the operating lease contract is signed, the lessor is not sure whether he or she will recover the capital and generate a return. There are future agreements to be negotiated and a sale of the assets to be determined.

Reasons for leasing

There are many reasons why organisations may prefer to lease plant and equipment rather than buy it. Here, we examine five principal ones.

(i)   A company may not have the funds available to purchase the assets or it may not have access to alternative sources of funds. On the other hand, the company may want to use funds available for other purposes, which could be more profitable, or where the acquisition of other assets cannot be achieved through the use of leasing. The acquisition of aircraft or ships tends to be very expensive while the purchase of computer facilities can be beyond the means of smaller companies. Hence, leasing is a source of finance and a way to enable the immediate use of assets upon payment of the first rental instalment.

(ii) There can be considerable tax advantages in leasing. For example, a lessor who owns the leased asset is able to deduct the associated capital allowance (depreciation) from taxable income. If the lessor can make better use of capital allowance tax shields than an asset's user can, it may make sense for the leasing company to own the equipment and pass on some of the tax benefits to the lessee in the form of lower lease payments. Companies which do not show taxable profits in the years prior to acquiring an asset may not be able to obtain the immediate advantages of any capital allowances. These companies can only obtain an early advantage of the investment tax allowances through leasing.

(iii) A company may not wish to own a certain type of asset, such as a computer. These assets tend to become obsolete very quickly, and the firm may always want to use the latest equipment. Lease arrangements allow the lessee to carry out this policy whilst avoiding the risks of selling second-hand IT equipment (at a cost of course).

(iv) Traditionally, leasing was seen as 'off-balance sheet' financing. Companies in the UK did not need to record leased assets together with other fixed assets on their balance sheets. Until 1976, financial leases were off-balance sheet financing under UK accounting principles. The only requirement was to add a brief note to the accounts describing the extent of lease obligations. This could affect the asset turnover ratio of the company. A company that leased its equipment could show a higher return on capital employed in its accounts than a company that purchased its fixed assets. If the earnings from using the asset exceeded the rental, a profit was shown. Also, under these earlier accounting rules, companies which leased appeared to have less debt than companies which borrowed to finance assets and apparently lower gearing ratios could put firms in a better light as far as *future* borrowing was concerned.

Accounting standards now typically require that all finance leases be capitalised, that is, the present value of the lease payments be shown

For example, Boots' operating leases on stores are off-balance sheet in this sense and this can affect performance such as price/book ratio and return

alongside the debt portion of the balance sheet. The leased asset must also be shown on the asset part of the balance sheet. However, the capitalisation of leased assets only applies to finance leases and not to operating leases. As a result, many companies structure their leasing deals so that they can be classed as operating leases and thus can be kept off the balance sheet, with the possible consequences of such 'window-dressing' to potential lenders and investors. Nevertheless, any such leasing arrangements should appear as a line in the income statement (Samuels *et al.*, 1995).

(v) Organisations whose nature is not profit-seeking do not have access to equity finance. Their access to debt finance may be limited either by central government controls or by banks and other lenders applying normal commercial risk criteria. Leasing offers an alternative source of funding for capital investment. Leasing was popular in UK local government in the 1970s and early 1980s because it allowed local politicians to get around rationing mechanisms imposed by central government through restrictions on borrowing. Central government closed this loophole by altering the tax provisions applying to capital allowances taken by lessors and then replacing controls on local authority borrowing by controls on expenditure.

'Lease v. buy and borrow' decision

We will deal next with the financial aspects of the 'lease v. buy and borrow' decision. Despite the non-quantitative reasons given above for undertaking a leasing arrangement, organisations also undertake an initial financial analysis of the two possible options to acquire an asset. The decision to be taken is 'lease, or buy and borrow'.

The choice between a finance lease and borrowing is complex, since the lease can be long-term in nature. Nevertheless, companies need to compare leasing with borrowing in order to choose the most cost-effective alternative on offer.

Although, as noted earlier, lessors are even more secure than secured lenders!

As stated above, a finance lease is effectively the same as debt capital in that, from a gearing standpoint, the present value of a lease contract liability is similar to the liability on debt finance. For simplicity, we also assume that the cost of capital is the same for purchasing and leasing because we noted that leasing is equivalent to secured debt finance. Box 5.1 illustrates one of the more traditional lease v. purchase analysis approaches.

BOX 5.1 LEASE V. BORROW

The problem

A company is considering a venture which requires the purchase of some plant. The machine costs £1,000 and will have a zero scrap value at the end of its three-year life.

The project is forecast to generate the following net cash flows (i.e. revenues less operating costs), pre-tax:

Year	Cash Flow (£)
1	+600
2	+550
3	+250

The plant could either be purchased outright or acquired through a finance lease. The lease contract requires three payments of £375, paid annually in advance.

We assume that the initial transaction is made on the last day of the previous accounting period and the firm expects to have a corporate tax liability throughout the next three years, against which it can offset any debt interest or lease payments.

Managers require that the project generate an after-tax return of at least 20%. This can be considered the appraisal discount rate.

The corporate tax rate is 35%, payable one year in arrears. Capital allowances for tax purposes of 25% on the reducing balance method are available on capital investments. The pre-tax cost of debt is 14%.

For a revision of the reducing balance method, see Section 4.4.3 of *Vital Statistics*.

The solution

The approach we adopt is to treat the decision as a two-stage process. First we compare the present value of the cost of leasing against purchasing and, second, evaluate the project using the least-cost method of purchase as the 'outlay'.

In the first stage, the after-tax cost of debt is used to reflect the low-risk nature of the cash flows and to take into account the tax-deductibility of debt. In the second stage, a discount rate is used which reflects the project's own systematic risk in this case 20%.

Stage one

After tax cost of debt: 14% (1− 0.35) = 9.1% = discount factor

PV of lease cash flows:

Year	Lease (£)	Tax Relief (£)		Discount Factor (9.1%)		(£)
0	−375		×	1.0000	=	−375.00
1	−375	+131.25	×	0.9166	=	−223.42
2	−375	+131.25	×	0.8401	=	−204.77
3		+131.25	×	0.7701	=	+101.88
	PV of lease payments				=	−702.11

PV of purchase cash flows:

Year	Outlay (£)	Capital tax allowance (£)		Discount Factor (9.1%)		(£)
0	–1,000		×	1.0000	=	–1,000.00
1		+87.50	×	0.9166	=	+80.20
2		+65.63	×	0.8401	=	+55.14
3		+49.22	×	0.7701	=	+37.90
4		+147.65	×	0.7058	=	+104.21
		PV of purchase			=	**–722.55**

Therefore it is cheaper to acquire the plant with a lease rather than to purchase.

Stage two

Project's NPV analysis

Year	PV cost (£)	Net cash flow (£)	Tax charge (£)		Discount factor 20%		(£)
0	–702.11			×	1.0000	=	–702.11
1		+600		×	0.8333	=	+499.98
2		+550	–210.00	×	0.6944	=	+236.10
3		+250	–192.50	×	0.5787	=	+33.28
4			–87.50	×	0.4823	=	–42.20
					NPV	=	**+25.05**

Therefore the project is worth undertaking by using a finance lease.

Source: adapted from Wilkes, Samuels and Greenfield (1996)

Summary

The choice of funding available to organisations has been discussed in this sub-section. We have focused on three types: equity, debt and leasing. A capital project can be funded by a combination of debt and equity, depending on a variety of factors. In addition, leasing has increasingly become a method of financing the purchase of plant, machinery, buildings, computers, aircraft and so on. We have examined the reasons for leasing and provided a numerical illustration of how a firm is able to make a lease v. purchase decision.

5.2 PROJECT FINANCE

This sub-section describes the specific issues relating to project finance, that is, the financing of large projects in the private sector.

Project finance can be defined as:

> '[The] financing of a project such that the lender is prepared to look only to the earnings of the project as the source of funds from which his loan will be repaid and to the assets of the project as collateral for the loan.'
>
> Nevitt and Fabozzi (1996)

As stated above, project finance is typically used to fund very large and often risky projects. A major concern for the project sponsors is to spread the inherent range of risks symptomatic of these types of projects. The sponsors are usually companies, such as oil and mining companies, which want to build, and at times operate, the project and intend to invest an amount of equity into the particular project.

Project finance is not exactly a newcomer to the finance scene. Indeed, in 1856, financing for the construction of the Suez Canal was raised by a variant of this technique. But is was not until some sixty years ago that early project finance techniques were used in the USA to fund the development of oilfields. Small Texan and Oklahoman wildcat explorers lacked sufficient capital to develop their oilfields and could not raise sufficient debt on their own credit standings. The banks developed a form of production payment finance – instead of looking at the companies' balance sheets for security, they relied on the specific oil reserves themselves with direct proceeds of oil sales earmarked for the loans' repayments.

A number of variations on this theme developed, but it was not until the expansion in North Sea oilfields that project finance grew beyond production payment financing and assumed some of the variety that it now has. Today, international banks provide project financing for a vast range of projects, including mineral developments, toll roads, tunnelling projects (such as the Channel Tunnel), theme parks, power stations, and shipping and aircraft finance.

Project finance is difficult to define exactly because there is no single technique that is immutably used – each financial facility is tailored specifically to suit the individual project and the needs of the parties sponsoring it. In essence, the expression 'project finance' describes a large scale, highly leveraged financing facility established for a specific undertaking whose creditworthiness and economic justification is based on the project's expected cash flows. It is the project's own economics rather than its sponsors' (in many cases the equity owners) financial strength that determines its viability. In this way, the sponsor isolates this activity, a method sometimes called **ring-fencing**, from its other business. Through careful structuring the sponsor may shift specific risk to project customers, developers and other participants, thus limiting its own financial risk.

This process of sharing risk is not without cost. Project financing is normally more expensive than conventional company debt (Buckley, 1998). The increased cost is caused by the identification of a whole range of risks which must be incorporated in any contract documentation. However, since project financing is normally highly leveraged, its overall cost of finance may be lower than a company's usual WACC.

Although many banks compete to fund projects and consequently the lending rates may go down, the large number of potential project contracts which banks consider and reject cause them additional expenditure on time and expert resources. But the ultimate result may be more acceptable to the sponsors, since, compared to direct funding, project finance is usually off-balance sheet and thus better reflects the actual legal nature of non-recourse financing.

In project finance terms, **non-recourse financing** occurs when lenders do not at any stage during the loan period, including the pre-production period, have recourse for repayment from other than project cash flows. In practice, such financing is almost unobtainable. Most projects are financed on a **limited recourse** basis, i.e. with a limited amount of recourse to sponsors and other parties.

The essential difference between non-recourse and limited-recourse finance occurs when a project is abandoned. In the non-recourse case, the sponsors can, in principle, walk away from the project without liability to repay the debt. Limited-recourse financing is a more accurate description of most project financing involving bank lenders. A wide range of arrangements exists which restrict the ability of lenders to look to project sponsors for repayment of debt in the event of problems with the loans. On completion of the project, lenders of both limited-recourse and non-recourse financing have recourse only to project cash flows and assets, if the project is designated as non-recourse at that point.

Figure 5.1 illustrates the complexity of the range of parties and factors which interact and are interdependent of each other in the process of project finance.

Lenders are attracted to project finance because they receive high fees compared with other business transactions they undertake. They are protected from interest and capital repayment default by a range of covenants from the sponsor and other parties. Spreading specific project

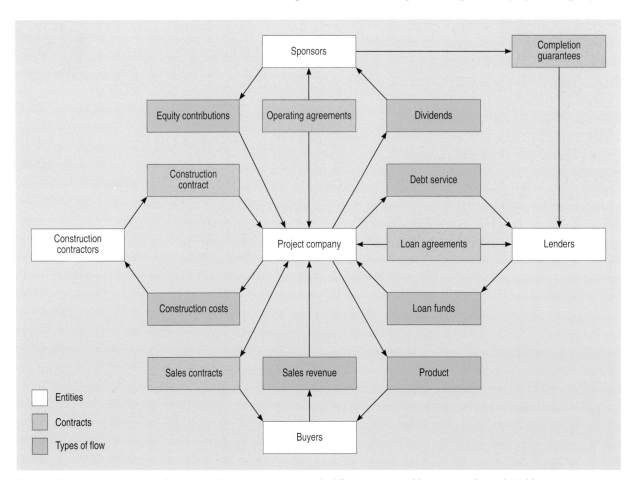

Figure 5.1   Project finance borrowing through a project subsidiary supported by sponsor's undertakings (Buckley, 1996)

risk over several participating lenders lessens dependence on a single sponsor's own credit standing.

BOX 5.2   THE CHANNEL TUNNEL

An example where project financing did not entirely go according to plan is the Channel Tunnel, the tunnel linking Southern England with Northern France. Despite the fact that the completed project represents a pinnacle of engineering and technological achievement, the issues of its financing are as yet far from resolved. As with all projects of this magnitude it appears that its main impetus was a political one, in this case an agreement between France and the UK. This in turn influenced the financial vehicles which were established to fund the tunnelling project. Because of the many unknown factors during the planning and construction phases, enormous cost and time overruns were experienced. The project's completion was delayed by a number of years and its cost escalated twofold to an estimated £8bn (at 1996 values). As a result the tunnel's actual cash flow profiles were completely different from those which were originally estimated. Nevertheless, by 1997, after the tunnel had been in operation for about two years, and despite a disastrous fire which rendered it inoperative to most rail freight traffic for about six months, the operational cash flows had become more or less acceptable to the lenders, subject to assurances of significant growth, despite the fact that at one stage the tunnel operating company suspended paying the interest charges on the loan capital.

The Channel Tunnel programme financial arrangements were completed long before the PFI began. PFI specialists argue that its funding structure was doomed because there was a conflict between sponsors and contractors – a duality of roles. Contractors effectively acted as sponsors as they did not get their money at the beginning, so their commitment to complete the project was minimal.

The funding of the tunnel also turned out to be a nightmare for the equity investors and the providers of debt capital. The numerous refinancing deals between the operating company and the approximately 250 syndicated banks were difficult to achieve. Court cases are still pending brought by equity investors against senior management.

Nevertheless, it is held that the banks, who complained bitterly about the range of refinancing arrangements which have taken place, received a good 'spread' on the loans as well as obtaining a 'free' additional equity holding. In the long term the project may well prove to be a good deal for the banks.

While specific features distinguish project finance from conventional corporate borrowing they may not all be present in a particular project. These features include:

- The project is usually established as a distinct, separate entity.
- It relies primarily on debt financing. Borrowings generally provide 70% to 80% of the total capital with the balance being equity contributions or subordinated loans from the sponsors. Some projects have been successfully structured with over 90% debt, but only in very special cases (this point highlights that projects funded through PFI and project financing have comparable financial structures).

PFI projects are discussed in Section 5.4.

'He's in conference at the moment about raising investment funds.'

- The project loans are linked directly to the venture's assets and potential cash flow.

- The sponsor's guarantees to lenders do not, as a rule, cover all the risks. Some sponsors may also be 'off-takers' (see Section 5.3) and, as a result, may also be subject to project post-completion risks.

- Firm commitments by various third parties, such as suppliers' performance guarantees, purchasers of the project's output, government authorities providing planning permission etc., and the project sponsors themselves, are obtained and these create significant components to support the credit financing of the project.

- The debt of the project entity is often completely separate from the sponsor companies' direct obligations.

- The lenders' security usually consists only of the project's assets, apart from project cash generation.

- The finance is usually for a longer period than normal bank lending.

Project finance is most frequently used in capital-intensive projects, such as in the case study which follows in Section 5.3. These projects are expected to generate strong and reasonably certain cash flows which are consequently able to support high levels of debt.

The inherent complexities of undertaking a project finance investment are extreme. You may find it helpful to refer back to Figure 5.1 to get an overview of the inter-relating variables and parties which constitute a typical project finance deal.

Finally, the critical part of the lender's analysis embraces a view on the risks of the project. We broadly identify two risk categories, although they can vary with the different types of organisation or even the types of projects.

Internal risks – which include:

- operating risk
- raw material handling risk
- completion (or construction risk)

Externally derived risks – which include:

- country/political risk
- off-take risk
- market risk
- financial risks, including foreign exchange risk
- documentary risk
- *force majeure* risk

Activity 5.1 _____

The above list states a rather comprehensive range of risks. Try to provide a short description of each of these risks in the context of project financing. If need be, base the definitions on the various risks to which your own organisation is exposed.

The above lists give an indication of the range of risks the providers of capital for projects must consider. At this stage, it is necessary only to obtain a general appreciation of the concept of such risks. The topic will be dealt with in more depth in Block 4. The following case narrative refers to these risk issues in the context of project finance. The following case study illustrates how organisations manage project financing risks in order to quantify them and to minimise them. We also show how project sponsors diversify away a number of project risks.

5.3 LIQUID GAS FACILITY IN OMAN CASE STUDY

This case study describes a specific example of project financing, the funding of a liquid gas facility in Oman an oil-rich state in the Persian Gulf.

The narrative of the case study is centred on the complex issues in the decision-making and negotiating processes to which every new project proposal will be subject. The topics are discussed from the viewpoint of the principal banks, and if any biases become apparent in the discussion they may be considered in this environment. The story is presented approximately in the order of the various steps of the decision-making processes. So, many activities take place simultaneously, in the various locations of the financial institutions, while the timing of some tasks cannot be determined. In any event, this should not detract from the description of the decision-making process.

In order to place the range of activities in their context it is helpful to obtain an overview of the structure of the project finance functions in ABN-Amro. The bank's structure is as follows:

- Independent Finance Units of which Project Finance is the largest
- Additional divisions which provide support are:
  Industry Group
  Export Group
  Structures Group
  Syndication Group

- The Project Finance unit has subdivisions including:
  Natural Resources
  Energy Finance (Oil/Gas)

Project funding arrangements

Project funding arrangements follow a well-established pattern. The project risks related to the gas facility project, of which more later, are deemed too high even for large banks and are diversified. The diversification of risk is done through a syndication procedure and is akin to the manner in which insurance companies reinsure their risks to a range of other insurance companies. This reinsurance of risk has been in operation in the UK for many years, for example through Lloyds syndicates, and has simply been copied by the banks in the case of the funding of large and costly projects.

In all large projects, the principal banks, called **arranging banks**, underwrite the funding for the project. In the Oman project, which cost about $2bn, the arranging banks were ABN-Amro, the largest Dutch bank which operates globally, and NatWest Bank which is involved in large projects all over the world in energy, power and telecommunications.

The loan for this project was syndicated to seven banks. These banks in turn sub-syndicated part of their funding commitment to a further 43 syndicate banks, making 50 banks in total. The choice of these banks is typically based on a range of factors, including:

- syndicate banks which are known to be interested in project finance for specific types of project
- banks which are experienced in specific countries/industries and have a track record in these areas.

The general rule is that the principal arranging banks take on a significant part of the total amount funded, although this depends on the amount of the loan. The largest amount funded by any member of this syndicate was about $75m, for both ABN-Amro and NatWest, and the lowest was about $2m.

However, the maximum amount of $75m was re-financed in the so-called secondary market. This market consists of smaller banks which were not invited into the original lending syndicate. It is held that these arrangements offer opportunities to improve the return on capital for the original syndicate. It is possible to refinance the total amount of funding to the secondary market but this is subject to the following conditions:

- It is usually done with the borrower's consent, based on agreement with the original funding syndicate in general and the arranging banks in particular.

- Borrowers and syndicate banks alike prefer the arranging banks to remain part of the loan syndicates, thus demonstrating their commitment, as well as for prestige and other credibility reasons.

The decision-making process

Before deciding to underwrite large projects, such as that in Oman, ABN-Amro conducts a range of financial analyses. A large part of this decision-making process is concerned with evaluating the risks involved, and is done by so-called 'modelling' banks or external contractors as well as by in-house specialist staff. These modelling banks provide a complete financial model of the proposed project and their models allow for a wide range of factors which might impinge on the project.

After the models have been completed and analysed, these are audited by independent groups of experts appointed by the arranging banks.

The analysis includes:

- Project base case scenario (based on the most reasonable assumptions known and ascertainable at the time the model is being constructed). Tests are then performed to check the robustness of the assumptions in the model. The model examines a range of ratios in relation to the project. For example the debt service history of the project's sponsors will be reviewed as well as their debt/equity ratios. In any event all sponsors must show commitment to the project by injecting a predetermined percentage of equity into the project.

- DCFs of the proposed project are calculated based on a whole range of financial forecasts, for such variables as interest rates, foreign currency exchange rates, and their sensitivities tested (sensitivity and scenario analysis).

As noted above, the recognition and appraisal of risk forms a major part of the decision-making process. The largest concern of the lending banks is to recognise the risks and manage them through an array of well-tried measures. However, the spreading of risks has costs: for example, refinancing the Oman project reduces the total profit available to the arranging banks. Nevertheless, given the size of the project, it is imperative that the overall risk of lending is reduced by the underwriting banks, in this case ABN-Amro and NatWest.

The following sub-sections describe a range of risks which were considered for the Oman liquid gas facility. They are included in the lists of internal and external risks earlier in this section.

Completion risk

This type of risk embraces technical risk, which depends on the type of technology used in the project. For example, has the proposed technology been used before or is the project based on new technology? Technical risk is dependent on the available skills and expertise in the host country. In practice, the banks allocate dedicated finance to complete the project. The pre- and post-completion loan structures are different, because they are linked to different risk profiles, as the banks perceive pre- and post-completion risks to be totally different.

This occurred with the delivery of Northern Line trains to LT (see Box 5.3).

During the construction stages of the project the contractors provide certain **completion guarantees** which are released against completion certificates. In the case of completion difficulties the banks can call in certain of the completion guarantees.

Country/political risk

The banks view this category as the most important risk factor in these types of project. Country risk is closely associated with political risk. In addition to examining purely economic assumptions one must look at:

- fiscal conditions in the host country (Oman)
- the investment climate based on the range of investments which have taken place in Oman
- the ability to repatriate funds – the current climate and the likely policies of future governments (see Section 3.5)
- the stability of government (if the government is a partner, examine issues such as guaranteed funds for the project, working capital and other sources of funds needed in the host country)
- political risk also refers to attitudes of consumers, customers, the general population, etc.

The pricing of political risk in the financing of a project is based on the characteristics of each country in which the project is taking place. The costing of the risk in the market is based on precedents in deals with that country. Difficulties naturally arise when no previous dealing or projects have taken place. The banks will then be more hesitant when looking at the risk profiles under which the loans will take place. However, there exist national risk ratings, similar to those provided for companies by Moody's, etc. The pricing of these risks changes with the stages of the project's implementation based on information provided by each bank's economic department usually in association with Moody's, Standard & Poors or IBCA. In addition, *The Economist* regularly provides tables which estimate country risks.

Table 5.1 shows the risk rating of a number of countries. These ratings are subjective scales that bear no direct numerical relationship to downside risk. Nevertheless, the table illustrates a number of comparative risks. In general, country risk ratings correspond closely to the risk of the country's government debt (measured by the premium over US Treasury bonds, for example).

See Units 4 and 8 for explanations of bonds, bond yields and interest rate risk.

Lessard (1996) points out: 'Country risk ratings, unfortunately, cannot be translated directly into cash flow or discount-rate adjustments since they are ranked on arbitrary dimensions'.

In some cases, political risk can be hedged with export credit agencies. These agencies guarantee, at a price, the payment to home country suppliers of goods and services sold to foreign customers, in the event that these customers default on paying for these goods and services. These have an

Table 5.1   Estimates of country risk

Country	Political risk (100)	Financial risk (50)	Economic risk (50)	Composite rating (100)
Algeria	50.0	36.0	28.5	57.0
Myanmar	58.0	28.0	30.5	58.0
Russian Federation	60.0	32.0	34.0	63.0
Philippines	62.0	39.0	36.0	68.5
Brazil	64.0	34.0	32.5	65.0
Mexico	65.0	41.0	31.5	69.0
India	66.0	37.0	36.5	70.0
Indonesia	67.0	40.0	37.5	72.0
China, P.R.	68.0	38.0	39.5	73.0
Thailand	75.0	44.0	41.0	80.0
Argentina	76.0	36.0	35.5	74.0
Malaysia	78.0	44.0	42.0	82.0
Chile	80.0	43.0	40.5	82.0
Korea, Republic	81.0	46.0	41.0	84.0
Taiwan	82.0	48.0	42.5	86.0
United States	83.0	48.0	38.5	85.0
Japan	86.0	48.0	44.0	89.0
Singapore	87.0	48.0	45.0	90.0

Source: The Economist

important, if not a vital, role in the area of country/political risk insurance. Of course, these agencies charge premiums on the amount of funds which are to be guaranteed under the agreements between the various parties of the project, and their charges are related to *their* perception of country/political risk. Likewise, part of the political risk can be insured.

The legal framework of the host country forms a major consideration in the decision-making process. For example, does local legislation support the local project partners to the detriment of outside lenders? Brazil, Egypt and many other countries do not recognise legal frameworks and decisions made in courts outside the their own jurisdiction. Similarly, countries such as Indonesia do not have legal systems which allow foreign banks easy recourse to repayment in the event of a default.

Finally, the involvement of the International Finance Corporation (IFC), which forms part of the World Bank, is considered in the management of country risk, particularly for countries perceived to have relatively large country/political risk. This organisation supports some private-sector projects, as it did the one in Oman, and is often willing to accept a different risk profile from that of normal lenders. This in turn provides a reduction in risk for the lending banks.

IFC, as part of their financial involvement could provide:

- a loan – direct to the project in question (this happens rarely)
- a syndicated loan to a group of bankers under the IFC umbrella. This in turn gives a measure of comfort to the lending banks. As a result a large portion of the political risk is deemed to be diversified away
- an equity stake in the project.

Off-take risk

Off-take risk, applicable to utility supply projects, is essentially the risk of guaranteeing purchase from the customers, wherever these customers might be. This risk is dependent on the number of countries which are involved with the project and its markets and is linked to commercial risk. The off-taker signs a contract with the project to buy the product. Thus the cash flows depend on the perception of the creditworthiness of the off-taker, which in turn is a function of location and financial strength. In the Oman project the main customer for the liquid gas is Korea. Hence the political risk analysis for this project included an evaluation of the risks associated with both Oman and Korea in order to provide the lenders with a more complete picture.

Market risk

The project's ability to generate cash streams to service the interest payments and the ultimate redemption of the capital outlay depends on the principle that the output of the project can be sold over the life of the project. The risk is obvious, even though, for example, oil and gas price changes can usually be predicted for the 2–5 year period ahead. However, many large projects have a long life span, so what will happen if the market collapses or the prices fluctuate wildly after the 2–5 years? There is a range of risk management instruments, derivatives, available which are able to manage market risk. Finally, the legal agreements between parties in project financing contain clauses which are concerned with these matters.

As you will see in Block 4, financial markets give a good indication of these through what are known as forward prices.

Financial statement issues for the lending banks

This subsection describes the treatment of the income streams in the profit and loss accounts and balance sheets of the banks. The level of income depends on the role of each syndicated bank in the funding process, as the income streams of the various lenders are based on a complicated range of fee structures. ABN-Amro and Natwest as the arranging banks receive the bulk of the fees which include:

(i) an arrangement fee

(ii) a fee for underwriting the project

(iii) a participation fee – this is a flat fee and received in advance

(iv) the loan spread – this is the percentage (points) above the base lending rate

(v) a commitment fee on the undrawn portion of the total amount to be financed

(vi) technical bank fee (this could be paid to the arranging bank or any other bank which specialises in the technical issues of the project and its lending procedures)

(vii) an administrative role fee – to the arranging bank only.

All syndicated banks receive one or more of these fees, based on the degree of their involvement in the project's funding. In addition, if these banks offer a particular expertise to the project and its planning, an additional fee can be negotiated.

As a rule the project sponsors' returns are based on a required return on equity capital. However, the banks are also interested in the return on debt capital which is based on the predicted income streams of the project over the life of the loan. All banks have a **main-requirement** under the 'capital adequacy requirement directive' (Basel Accord, 1988) and determine their required return within the constraints of this accord. It is common practice that banks do not set a *hurdle rate* for project financing. The most important consideration is the evaluation of the risks involved with the particular project for which the funds are provided.

It is interesting to note that *no* standard pricing of any loan agreement exists. This means that the system of costing a loan, i.e. the interest rate applied, is different from one project to another. These rates are based on a whole range of factors which banks take into consideration when analysing each project proposal.

In all cases the balance sheets of the banks must report the amount of debt funded. The disclosure in the balance sheet is itemised depending on the specific amount underwritten, in which context these amounts are underwritten, as well as the time scales of the project.

Typically, large projects are highly leveraged with a debt/equity ratio of approximately 70/30 or 80/20. These large loans form an important part of the banks' balance sheet profile.

The Annual Report must explain in the notes how the banks reported the following items in the balance sheet:

- commitment to lend (intention to lend to the project)
- the total capital requirement for the project
- the total funds dedicated to the project, but not yet lent to the borrower.

The total funds intended for the project appear as assets on the balance sheet.

Note that loans appear on the balance sheet as *assets* for banks, whereas they are *liabilities* for the companies taking out the loans.

5.4   THE PRIVATE FINANCE INITIATIVE

Public services, in the United Kingdom and in most, if not all, countries in the world, often face service demands they cannot meet for want of infrastructure and/or facilities. This may be due to a shortage of finance in the sense that public borrowing is constrained by macroeconomic policies. As part of an attempt to alleviate this situation, many governments around the world are encouraging the use of private investment in services traditionally provided by the public sector. In the UK, this is currently being done through what is known as the **Private Finance Initiative (PFI)**. PFI can be described officially as follows:

> The PFI has become one of the Government's main instruments for delivering higher quality and more cost-effective public services. Its aim is to bring the private sector more directly into the provision of public services, with the public sector as an enabler and, where appropriate, guarding the interest of the users and customers of public services. It is not simply about the financing of capital investment in services, but about exploiting the full range of private sector management, commercial and creative skills.
>
> HM Treasury (1995)

In its simplest form, PFI and similar Public Private Partnership (PPP) schemes in Britain allow public bodies to contract directly with private sector organisations for the provision of capital finance. The private sector organisation accepts some of the project's risk in return for an operator's licences to provide specified services with a view to making a profit and hence a return on equity. The private sector **operator** generates this return on equity through the revenue stream arising from the services. The **operator**, such as a housing, healthcare, security or welfare organisation, is usually part of a **consortium** that may include construction companies and banks, which bids for projects in competition with other consortia. The consortium which obtained the contract to build and run the Altcourse Prison, a case illustrated in Video Programme 1, consists of a group of companies which possess the relevant expertise in building and running a project of this size, as well as a group of banks involved in the funding of the project.

Activity 5.2 _____

Watch Video Programme 1 'Public project, private finance', and link the events taking place in the film to the theory and practice described in this section of the unit.

The concept of public-sector investments being funded by the private sector is not new (see Box 5.3).

BOX 5.3   THE SOUTH SEA BUBBLE

The South Sea Company (1711) offered to take on the [British] Government debt in return for a monopoly in trading in the South Sea. The company would have exclusive rights over trade with the east of South America from the Orinoco to Tierra del Fuego, and along the whole of the west coast. The underlying reason for this new company was to take over some of the government's debt, as England was nearly broke after too many wars. The debt, £9 million, was to be serviced at a rate of 6% per annum secured on the duties payable on wines, vinegars, tobacco, wrought silks and whalefins. The company's original issues of shares at par, i.e. £100 of stock was sold for £100, but it was not until four years later that the price of the shares traded in the coffee houses of the City actually rose to that level. This was because of the poor view the public took of the government's debt. No wonder, as there was rather too much of it – and some would say it has been that way ever since. After eight years, when the company did virtually no business, the shares became the subject of a speculative rush. Everybody was buying South Sea shares, including the Prince of Wales, Robert Walpole, MP's, nobles, including a great number of French nobles who were keen to make Mississippi-type profits in London.

At the height of the speculative madness, on June 24th 1720, the price of a £100 nominal share was £1050, with an estimated total market value of the shares in London of about £500 million. However, the bubble burst and on 28 September the price had fallen to £190 per share and there was a run on the Bank of England. The Bank of England and the East India Company jointly took over the South Sea Company which continued to trade but never successfully until it ceased to trade in 1748, but managed to continue as a name dealing in government securities for another hundred years.

One chronicler attributed the events to 'the overbearing insolence of ignorant men who had risen to sudden wealth by successful gambling'. Perhaps, but some of the best names in British society of the time were involved. In the words of one contemporary epigram:

'A wise man laughed to see an ass
Eat thistles and neglect good grass,
But had the sage beheld the folly
Of late transacted in Change Alley,
He might have seen worse asses there
Give solid gold for empty air.'

Murray (1985)

PFI projects typically have the following characteristics:

- The contractor provides the capital investment.
- The capital investment is funded by banks and other members of the consortium, possibly including the operators.
- The contractor assumes some of the venture's construction risks.
- The operator is awarded an operating licence for the capital facility to provide associated services, for example, prisons, hospitals and bridges and assumes these operating risks.
- The ownership of the facility is transferred to the private sector through the setting up of a separate company to build and run the project.

The attractions of PFI to a public body such as a local council can be considerable according to central government. For example:

- Its capital programme does not have to be constrained by central government controls on its expenditure and borrowing. In the UK, the ascendancy of monetarist economic policy has made government protective of limits on the **Public Sector Net Cash Requirement (PSNCR)** (see the hospital case study in Box 5.6).
- It can exploit the added value which specialist private-sector providers can bring through innovation, notably in design and quality of service.

PSNCR (formerly known as the Public Sector Borrowing Requirement PSBR) is the amount of the central government's budget deficit, i.e. the extra funding the government has to borrow to finance spending in excess of its income from taxes and other sources together with other borrowing by governmental organisations, including local education authorities and hospitals.

MEET THE FIRST PATIENTS ON OUR NEW PFI-FUNDED WING—TWO ACCOUNTANTS CAUGHT FIGHTING OVER WHETHER OR NOT WE ARE PART OF THE PSBR

ROGER BEALE

- Some of the long-term operating risk, such as higher maintenance costs for the facility or a less than predicted working life, can be transferred to the private-sector company which may be obliged to hand back the facility in working condition at the end of the (perhaps 25-year) contract. However, the transfer of the risk means that the annual expected cost to the public purse is higher than if the services were provided by the public sector.

Thus, the potential downside of the PFI is that the public sector may find itself gaining access to capital funding in the short term only by committing to pay out increasingly large shares of future revenue streams in the long term.

Potential consortia or contractors will appraise each PFI project using capital budgeting, as discussed in the earlier parts of this unit. However, the finance for a PFI project will usually be specific to the project and not provided from general resources available to the companies in the consortium. This is why banks are usually included in the bidding consortium and why private-sector firms treat investment in PFI projects as a type of project financing (see Section 5.2). The PFI project's costs and benefits are ring-fenced (i.e. separate and independent from the contractors' main business) and often a separate profit centre or division is created entirely devoted to funding and operating the facility for the length of the contract.

However, contractors must take into account a number of specific questions:

- Is finance available at the usual rates of interest?
- Is there a stable government policy environment in which the contractors can plan?
- What are the degrees of certainty, in the form of guarantees (especially to the revenue streams if they are vulnerable to the changing policy decisions of the public-sector user of the project)?

In addition to these questions, PFI projects are subject to a range of risks affecting all capital projects, and even with the most sophisticated forecasting procedures it is impossible to anticipate the outcome of future events. The range of risks runs from such items as design problems, variation in operating costs, volume changes over time, residual value and early cessation of the project. The probability, and the costs, of the risks must be ascertained by the bidding consortium and form part of their PFI project investment appraisal processes.

In order to deliver a PFI solution to a particular funding problem, a complex process needs to be undertaken. A public-sector body will have to determine exactly what the project is to be and state the timescales for completion. Projects may be to **design, build, finance and operate** (**DBFO**) a facility (e.g. Northern Line trains, Altcourse Prison), or may involve other variations, such as **build, operate and transfer** (**BOT**).

LT funding issues formed a key point of discussion during the run-up to the election of the Mayor for London in 2000.

The LT case study in Box 5.4 provides one example of the manner in which many large public-sector capital projects are likely to be funded in future. If LT intends to maintain its present level of service in addition to expanding the existing underground network, PFI funding is currently, according to the government, the only way of financing the investments required without recourse to full or partial privatisation. Critics of the government, however, claim that finance can be raised cheaply and easily by issuing bonds, as has been done to finance improvements to the New York subway.

BOX 5.4   FUNDING THE NORTHERN LINE REFURBISHMENT

The Northern Line (NL) is one of the busiest sections of the London underground network. It provides around 108 million passenger journeys per annum (some 15% of the total network in 1994/95). It generates some £100m in revenue and costs about £90m per annum to run. The line operates 50 stations, two rolling stock maintenance depots and employs 2,000 staff. In the mid-1990s the rolling stock consisted mainly of 1959 vintage trains, which were becoming increasingly unreliable and costly to maintain. For some considerable time the NL had been earmarked for major modernisation. The main benefits of the modernisation would include increased revenues, substantial passenger benefits and an opportunity to reduce costs.

A proposed refurbishment project included investment in new rolling stock. In addition, some existing rolling stock was to be renovated and stations and property modernised. Communications, signalling and other systems, such as power supply and escalators, were to be totally overhauled and the latest technology installed.

While planning the refurbishment project LT recognised the funding constraints imposed by central government. As a result LT had three options

- postpone the investment in new trains and infrastructure to a later date when funds might become available

- spend extra funds on the maintenance of the old trains and run the equipment for the foreseeable future

- investigate the opportunities provided by the PFI funding route.

LT management chose the last option.

In appraising the NL trains project, LT analysed PFI funding v. conventional funding for the rolling stock. The PFI rules dictate that risks are to be diversified away as much as possible. The PFI funding approach involved considering the risks attached to both alternatives. Under conventional funding, LT would bear the major risks such as train breakdowns and delays in receiving the new trains. Under the conditions of a 'good' PFI contract these risks could be transferred to the private sector in exchange for a probably higher return to the private sector consortium and hence a higher cost to LT.

LT emphasised that for the NL refurbishment it was seeking a complete service, with the private-sector supplier of the service taking on full responsibility for the design, manufacture, maintenance and cleaning of both trains and associated trackside equipment (e.g. closed circuit television). In December 1994, GEC-ALSTHOM was announced as the preferred bidder for the project, and the contract was signed in April 1995. It was expected that the trains would be delivered in a period from mid-1996 to late 1998. The GEC-ALSTHOM contract was subject to a range of penalty clauses, including compensation for the late delivery and consequent delayed operation of new rolling stock. These were invoked as delays were experienced. However, by 2000, the new trains were running as planned.

Figure 5.2 overleaf, illustrates the value for money trade-off through the symbolic use of a see-saw in order to highlight the balancing act private funders and the public sector have to go through before a PFI deal can be closed.

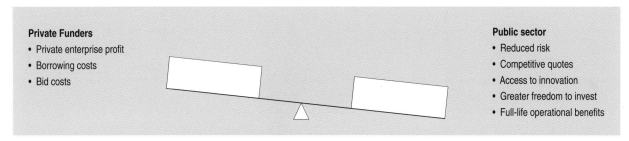

Figure 5.2   The value for money trade-off (CIMA Public Service Management, 1996)

PFI and PPP projects may be funded by a mixture of:

● government contribution, raised ultimately from borrowing or current taxes

● investment **special purpose vehicle (SPV)** (e.g. risk capital is invested in a new company formed specifically for the project). The SPV may be funded by a mixture of equity and debt.

Some organisations are discouraged from bidding because of the time it takes to put a PFI deal together. For larger projects this bidding process can take well over a year. Accordingly, staff costs for those involved with the project analysis and negotiation procedures can be substantial. In Video Programme 1, Dawn Stephenson, the Finance Director at the Calderdale Healthcare NHS Trust, refers to the lengthy discussions and time-consuming negotiations which took place before the PFI deal was concluded.

An important point to consider is that funding for a PFI project will typically be needed over a prolonged period of time. As such PFI deals are long-term, the usual way to reduce the risk burden is to borrow long-term at fixed rates. Banks and financial markets are beginning to adjust to this requirement, whereas in the past many lenders would not go beyond 15 years (Collins, 1997). Contracts are typically of 25–30 years' duration, reflecting their infrastructure nature.

The banks will expect some financial commitment from either or both the contractor and operator. The amount of the equity portion of the funding, in the UK, tends to be lower than that which applies to normal project finance – between 10% and 20% – depending on how the lenders rate the scheme. The Altcourse prison scheme is funded by £95.5m debt (£82.6m at a fixed rate of 9.095% for 15 years, and £12.9m at 1.5% over LIBOR), while Tarmac and Group 4 put in an equity stake of £4m each, constituting about an 8.4% equity level.

LIBOR – London Interbank Offered Rate.

If we compare typical PFI funding with how such projects were traditionally funded by the public sector, the reality has been that most capital outlays by government and local government have been funded by loans repaid over the operating life of assets used in the project. The interest and principal repayment have been made using taxes raised annually. Roughly speaking, taxpayers have funded projects/assets over their useful life, giving rise to something approaching **generational equity**, i.e. this year's taxpayers pay the cost of this year's services, so that tax revenues are not 'saved' up in order to fund future asset purchases, and debts are not run up to fund current expenditure and consumption.

PFI offers challenges of a non-financial nature, such as the attitudes and skills available in the organisational cultures of the parties concerned. The technical challenges presented by the PFI's contracting arrangements and risk transfer are of particular significance. Contractors have found that PFI makes demands well beyond the ability of in-house expertise. Certainly,

BOX 5.5 'SEVERN CROSSING SETS A PRECEDENT'

The Second Severn Bridge Crossing (across the Bristol Channel between Wales and Avon County) which opened in 1996 is regarded as a successful PFI project because it achieved two previously unheard of targets – it was built on time and within budget. Contractors and shareholders in the consortia were John Laing, the French GTM construction group, Bank of America which advised and arranged, and BZW. Arranging the finance were Credit Agricole and Lloyds Bank.

The new company, which won the concession for 30 years, took over the bridge project, with its debt and cash flow and all the outstanding government debt. The total capital cost for the project, known as a Boot (build, own, operate and transfer), was £700m. Of this, only £100,000 was equity, although just £50,000 was paid up.

The funding was structured as follows. The Government provided £60m of subordinated debt, to be repaid at the end of the project, as well as contributing a debenture loan of £130m. The Bank of America took the biggest tranche of the debt with £170m. Credit Agricole and Lloyds each took on £85m, which was then syndicated down. Typically, margins on projects like this are about 1% above Libor. The balance of around £170m was made up of existing funds and any surplus funds from the bridge. In many ways the Severn Crossing was modelled on the highly successful Dartford Tunnel [This actually consists of one tunnel and one bridge, Queen Elizabeth II Bridge, crossing the Thames east of London], which has to date exceeded all toll and traffic forecasts. So far the Severn, which opened in 1996, is also set to meet all of its projected targets.

Source: *The London Financial News*, 28 July–3 August, 1997

managers in the public sector have learned that they are often obliged to buy technical expertise, such as legal services, which add considerably to the cost of the deals.

Organisationally there are challenges of structure and process. For PFI these include long-term relationships (possibly up to 20 or 30 years) between the public sector and private entities who provide not just the original capital but also the operational services. Construction companies (often lead contractors) have found themselves having to adapt their structures and processes considerably in order both to be able to work within the complex alliance of the bidding consortium and to run the operations management of the contract as it passes through the various stages.

The final outcome of the lengthy negotiation process between private and public-sector parties should result in the following:

- the private sector will have injected a tranche of risk equity capital into an SPV

- the SPV will have assumed responsibility for raising the necessary additional funds from the private sector

- the SPV will provide the management and the expertise to manage the development efficiently and effectively and accept the risks – particularly of time and cost – which would previously have been borne by the public-sector body

- the open tendering procedure has enabled the foundation of a solid, committed and competitive contract

- use of public funding will have been delayed until the scheme is operational, and will then be of a revenue nature. Private borrowing will have replaced public borrowing

- the private sector will feel that the potential rewards of the deal are in line with the risks undertaken and these will be carefully managed.

A hospital case study

The following case study (Box 5.6), based on discussions with the managers of the John Radcliffe Hospital Trust in Oxford, illustrates some of the difficulties experienced by NHS providers when raising funding for capital projects in the health service environment. The NHS is the UK government health service. Under the planner-provider system, Districts within the national system purchase medical, ambulance and other services provided by local NHS Trusts and other providers. NHS Trusts were created as separate independently managed units which operate hospitals and other support services in a particular town, city or county.

Under PFI or PPP arrangements, public sector service provider responsibilities are shared with or transferred to the private sector, which secures its remuneration through prospective payments by NHS planner and funding organisations or through lease payments by NHS Trusts. There are a number of ways in which this can be done:

- private consortia finance, construct and own hospitals which are leased and operated by NHS trusts

- private consortia finance, construct and own hospitals in which they also provide non-clinical services (e.g. food and hotel services, laundry, transport) while clinical services (clinicians, nursing, pharmacy, laboratory, radiology) remain the responsibility of the relevant NHS trust

- the private sector tenders for contracts to provide services to NHS planning and funding organisations thereby bypassing NHS trusts.

BOX 5.6 CASE STUDY: THE NHS AND CAPITAL INVESTMENT

The UK central government has traditionally used cash accounting. Fixed asset purchases are expensed (treated as a cost) in the year of acquisition and therefore do not appear on the government's balance sheets. Such practices have been criticised as a potential source of poor accountability and of inefficiency, the latter on grounds that assets are regarded as "free" or having no opportunity cost. In response to this criticism, the government introduced *capital charging*, whereby public-service departments and providers must pay an annual charge on the assets under their control. This charge is based upon the value of these assets. The rationale is that ending the treatment of assets (and thereby capital) as a 'free good' will lead to improvements in productive efficiency: departments and similar providers will try to reduce the cost of charges by using fewer assets of less value.

The implementation of capital charging requires opening and closing valuations of the asset base and a measure of the 'wearing out' of assets during the period.

In sectors such as health care with long-lived, highly specific assets, historical cost is not only irrelevant but probably impossible to establish reliably, as records of the original cost of acquisition typically do not exist and are outdated in any case. Because the NHS dominates health care provision in the UK, there is almost no outside market for either hospitals or hospital enterprises, so that open market existing use value cannot be established.

In the NHS, use has therefore been made of depreciated replacement cost (DRC). In practice, all valuations of operational assets have proceeded on the basis of DRC, a process involving assessment by the District Valuer of the rebuilding cost of a like-for-like asset. However, recourse to DRC encounters a number of serious difficulties and, in practice, investment choices which look attractive under capital charging and DRC will not necessarily be those preferred under the discounted cash flow approach of minimising the present value of future costs.

Chief executives of NHS trusts and regional NHS planning and funding bodies are responsible for managing the preparation of business cases for capital investment for all regions (with support from consultant medical staff). It must be clear that there are sound cost-benefit reasons for any proposed investment and that clinician and other professional staff who would make use of the proposed facilities support the scheme in concept and are able and willing to afford its financial implications. Chief executives must ensure that this support is explicitly given by main users before a cost-benefit case can be submitted to the NHS Executive for approval.

The John Radcliffe NHS Trust, which consists of four hospitals in Oxford, has a turnover of £150m and a £10m annual capital charge. The total investment project allocation is limited by the NHS at £5m per annum. Schemes over £1m each have to be applied for separately. However, these schemes are subject to the availability of funds which for some years have been very constrained by central government. For this reason, PFI and similar alternative methods of acquiring new healthcare facilities have been employed by NHS Trusts. In April 1998, for example, the UK Government sanctioned 11 new projects on this basis.

So far the discussion in this section puts PFI in a favourable light. Despite the complexities of its implementation, such partnerships appear to provide substantial benefits for the public sector as well as the private sector. The following newspaper extracts highlight the teething problems experienced in some early PFI projects.

PFI BOSS HITS AT £100M WASTE ON NHS SCHEMES

More than £100m of taxpayers' money has been wasted on duplicated advice to PFI schemes in the National Health Service.

David Steeds, chief executive of the influential private finance panel executive, said the money wasted on duplicated legal and financial advice could be massively cut by better oversight of projects.

His figures are three times higher than earlier estimates and come as the Treasury [government finance department] considers a review of the PFI completed last week.

Steeds warned that bankers and lawyers are poised to cream off similar sums as the PFI is extended to areas such as local authority projects and schools.

He said: 'Banks and lawyers have offered the same advice to different NHS Trusts across the country and there has been massive duplication. There could have been huge savings if Trusts had communicated better and if the process had been more closely co-ordinated from the top'.

Source: *Financial Mail on Sunday,* June 15, 1997

An even weightier critic, the National Audit Office, criticised a major PFI project, the Skye bridge:

PFI AND SKYE BRIDGE

'It raised doubts about the whole basis for deciding on PFI schemes. Its report into the £23m Skye bridge [between mainland Scotland and the Island of Skye], the first of the series into different aspects of the PFI, queried the Scottish Office's failure to compare the bridge with the alternative of improving the facilities of the existing ferry service'.

Source: *Financial Times*, 17 July, 1997

Activity 5.3

Read Case Study 4, 'Making the right financial connections for Melbourne', in the Course Reader. This shows how PFI and project finance projects are the same the world over.

SUMMARY

In this section we considered how capital projects can be funded, and whether the chosen method of finance makes any difference. We considered sources of funds available to public sector, private sector and regulated utilities.

Equity- and debt-funding topics were touched upon, although they have been described in earlier units. As leasing is an important method of financing plant and equipment it is necessary to understand the costs as well as the opportunities that this type of funding offers.

Project financing has the advantage to a borrower that a separate entity is set up and hence the debts arising from the project may not be recorded on the balance sheet; in other words the financing is 'off-balance sheet' from the borrower's point of view. However, project financing can be costly to arrange, and may be as simple to arrange as a direct loan.

Finally, a relatively new development in the method of funding public projects is the Private Finance Initiative (PFI) – private-sector funding, and possibly running, of public-sector projects, such as building a prison, providing new underground trains, or managing hospital services.

6 CAPITAL RATIONING

So far we have implicitly assumed that all project proposals which have a positive NPV should be sanctioned, funded and implemented. In this section we examine why an organisation may not be able to undertake all investment projects it may want to because of a shortage of investment funding. Organisations may also face other constraints and practicalities which force them to make choices between competing projects.

We examine the issues surrounding the shortage of investment capital to which most, if not all, organisations are subject most of the time. Capital rationing issues involve the selection of an optimal array of investment projects under financial and other resource constraints. We make the distinction between 'hard' and 'soft' capital rationing. We discuss competing projects and the 'make or buy' decision, where an organisation has the opportunity to outsource its production or services as opposed to producing their products in-house. In the same context we review aspects of competing projects. We expand the issues further by examining the private sector question of whether a company should grow organically or through the acquisition route.

6.1 CAPITAL RATIONING IN PRACTICE

A **capital rationing** problem is defined as a situation where there are insufficient funds to finance all potentially beneficial projects, whether benefit refers to profit or public service. A distinction is often made between hard and soft capital rationing. **Hard capital rationing** arises when the constraints are *externally* determined, such as providers of capital or government controls. **Soft capital rationing** arises with *internal*, management or governing body imposed, limits on investment expenditure.

A major problem which faces many organisations is cash shortage. For example, we have seen that many public-sector organisations are constrained by central government ideology and policy from raising loan finance. If an organisation identifies several projects that are beneficial (i.e. have a positive NPV or benefits which outweigh costs), it would like to undertake all of them. However, it may be prevented from doing so through a lack of funds. The restriction is a practical one. In theory, if a profit-oriented project proposal shows a positive NPV, there should be no problem raising the cash for its implementation. A positive NPV indicates how much better off a business would be after adequately rewarding all suppliers of capital.

The Profitability Index method is discussed in detail in Section 4.4.4 of *Vital Statistics*.

In practice, however, a business will find its capital rationed for a number of internal or external reasons. The organisation must choose which projects to invest in so that its objectives are met as fully as possible. In addition, an organisation may also be constrained by its inability to manage all projects it would like to undertake – in other words, management skills themselves are also a scarce resource.

There are a number of techniques available to enable management to decide, in principle, which projects can be undertaken under conditions of a shortage of investment capital. We will illustrate one such method, called the **profitability index (PI)** or **cost–benefit index** method. It has its limitations, but is a useful instrument to assist management in their decision-making tasks.

Let us look at the following simple example:

A firm has a cost of capital of 10% and has the option of three investment proposals, outlined in Table 6.1.

Table 6.1				
Project	Investment (£m) T_0	Inflows (£m) T_1	Inflows (£m) T_2	NPV (£m)
A	−10	+30	+5	+21
B	−5	+5	+20	+16
C	−5	+5	+15	+12

All three projects are attractive, but the firm has a limit on its CAPEX spending of £10m, so it can invest either in project A or in projects B and C, but not in all three. Although individually B and C have lower NPVs than project A, when added together their NPVs are higher.

The PI is expressed by the following simple formula:

$$PI = \frac{\text{Net present value}}{\text{Investment}}$$

For the three above projects the PI can be calculated as in Table 6.2.

Table 6.2	Profitability index		
Project	Initial investment (£m) at T_0	NPV (£m)	PI
A	−10	+21	2.1
B	−5	+16	3.2
C	−5	+12	2.4

Project B has the highest PI and C the next highest. Therefore, if our CAPEX budget limit is £10 million, we should accept these two project proposals. When projects have positive NPVs they will also have positive PIs. All projects with a positive PI would be acceptable, but where choices have to be made the magnitudes can determine a ranking of projects.

However, there are limitations to the use of PI under certain circumstances, such as when resources are constrained over more than one period, or when two proposed projects are mutually exclusive or when one project is dependent on another. Nevertheless, the simplicity of PI does allow for rankings to be established in many situations.

A more complex capital rationing problem is illustrated by the following example. Let us look at Table 6.3:

Table 6.3 Multi-period capital rationing		
Years	Project A Present value of cash flows (£)	Project B Present value of cash flows (£)
0	(8,000)	(6,000)
1	(4,000)	(8,000)
2–5 cumulative inflows	28,000	29,000
NPV @ 10%	16,000	15,000

Note that each project needs funding in two periods and each produces a positive NPV when discounted at 10%. If there were no shortage of funds both projects should be undertaken, as both are worthwhile.

Assume, however, that only £10,000 is available at time 0. Assuming that projects must be undertaken as a whole or not at all, project A should be chosen as it will produce an NPV of £16,000. Although project B uses up only £6,000 of the funds at time 0, whereas project A consumes £8,000, we have no other project on which to spend leftover cash and merely leaving it in the bank earning interest at or below the discount rate will give a zero, or even a negative, NPV.

This discussion about capital rationing by no means covers the subject in full. The problem of investment decision-making in the face of capital rationing over more than one period is both complex and, at present, not completely resolved. We have described a number of decision rules to determine the best use of scarce investment capital and how best to select projects which generate the highest positive NPV. In addition, we can apply sensitivity analysis to the range of relevant cash flows, of the comparative projects, and use the results to decide which project to select.

In the public sector, managers also have to choose between competing projects where criteria other than positive NPVs may also be relevant. The 'bottom lines' of public service projects include such criteria as the ability to defend and attack; the ability to keep order; the ability to educate the young and the not-so young; and the ability to keep people and products on the move. One could argue that benefit-cost techniques provide a quantitative equivalent to NPV, but applying a benefit-cost approach may involve inputting values on keeping people alive, having people educated to certain standards, protecting people and property from wrongdoers, or shortening travelling times. These inputted values, apart from being technically and socially controversial ('who can put a value on human life?'), may give a spurious quantitative accuracy to analyses which are entirely subjective. In the end, it is often up to politicians, government administrators and professional people employed in government (soldiers, doctors, teachers, social workers, engineers) to reach subjective decisions through co-operative, competitive/political and

An example of the public sector inputting values to services is LT s valuation of customers benefits from shorter travelling times, discussed in Section 3.3 of this Unit.

democratic means, using criteria which are social and economic as well as political.

Activity 6.1 _____

Distinguish between hard and soft capital rationing and describe examples in your own organisation of each of the two categories.

6.2 COMPETING PROJECTS

This sub-section deals with the choice organisations must make in the case of competing projects which, for example, offer a specific output but use a different technology to achieve this output. We will also describe the situation when an organisation has to determine if it is profitable to invest in, for example, additional plant and machinery, or buy in the products from an outside supplier. This classic problem in the application of DCF methods is known as the '**make or buy**' problem. It illustrates the way that opportunity costs can be taken into account within a single project DCF framework.

Let us first deal with competing projects. We can distinguish a range of circumstances when this condition applies, such as:

- projects competing for funds and resources within one organisation or between organisational divisions
- projects competing for internal or external markets, overlapping resources, e.g. technology shared between divisions.

Particularly in large organisations, management may have a range of options in their capital investment portfolio. A company could operate in various countries and management must choose where to produce its products, or indeed how to serve its markets in the best way. Competing projects can be taken a step further, whereby project proposals have to compete for funds available in the corporate investment budgets. The proposals may be ranked according to the corporate need. In this context you could get involved in the internal political issues and lobbying of divisional managers, described in Lumijärvi (1992).

A correct 'make or buy' decision can often be a major determinant of profitability. However, there is some evidence that many organisations have no basis for evaluating the make or buy decision. Blaxill and Hout (1991) found that many firms make outsourcing decisions primarily on the basis of overhead costs. The choice of which components to outsource is made by ascertaining what will save most on overhead costs, rather than on what makes the most long-term economic sense. In the public sector, outsourcing has found favour as a means of cost cutting, as labour provided by the private sector may entail lower costs and related employee benefits.

Another argument for outsourcing is often stated to be the rapid changes in the market and the lack of flexibility that characterises in-house production. However, this tendency to outsource components or services which were formerly performed in-house can result in unexpected cost increases, with many organisations failing to integrate the 'make or buy' decision into the overall business strategy. This can lead to a situation where manufacturing processes or services are dispersed at random throughout the organisation's operations and facilities and it becomes dependent on a much wider range of suppliers of components and services. An additional risk is that management can lose control over its operations and output and hence severely put the company's cash flows at risk. This is in contradiction to the original objective of outsourcing in order to save costs.

However, despite the possible drawbacks of outsourcing, the 'make or buy' decision has become a widely discussed business issue and it must be considered in this context. In the case of manufacturing it would simply be a choice of either making components in-house or buying them from an outside source. We can apply the same principle to retailers, where the company could invest in new shops and develop these outlets and their markets or buy an established chain of stores to expand their retail market. They are in fact buying market share.

The costs of achieving the above objectives have a different structure in each case. The 'make or buy' decision can often be formulated as an investment appraisal problem. Even so, there are some important factors which are not quantifiable, for example the security of supply if the firm has outsourced its supplies.

> For simplicity we have ignored tax in this example. A cost-saving project typically has tax implications in the same way as a revenue-generating project.

BOX 6.1 DELTA

Delta is considering producing a component in-house that it needs in an assembly operation. Its manufacture requires additional plant costing £400,000 which would last for four years with a residual value of £200,000. Manufacturing costs in each year would be £500,000, £700,000, £800,000 and £900,000 respectively. If Delta outsources the components the costs are forecast to be £900,000, £1,000,000, £1,100,000 and £1,400,000 in each year. However, the plant will occupy floor space which can be put to other uses generating £200,000 in each of the four years. This opportunity is lost if the 'make' option is adopted. If the WACC is 13%, should Delta make or buy the component?

The costs associated with making in-house (net of residual value in the final year) are:

(All amounts in £)

t = 0	t = 1	t = 2	t = 3	t = 4
400,000	500,000	700,000	800,000	700,000

The costs associated with buying in the components are:

t = 0	t = 1	t = 2	t = 3	t = 4
0	900,000	1,000,000	1,100,000	1,400,000

Thus the *gross* savings in costs if the components were made rather than outsourced are:

t = 0	t = 1	t = 2	t = 3	t = 4
(400,000)	400,000	300,000	300,000	700,000

The income forgone by occupying floor space if the 'make' decision is taken should be deducted from these savings. This leaves the cash flow changes due to making the component in-house as:

t = 0	t = 1	t = 2	t = 3	t = 4
Opportunity cost of plant floor space				
0	200,000	200,000	200,000	200,000
Savings of making less opportunity cost				
(400,000)	200,000	100,000	100,000	500,000

The NPV of the above cash flow streams can now be calculated as follows:

Year	Cash flow (previous table)	Discount factor	Present value of cost savings of make v. buy
t = 0	(400,000)	1.0	(400,000)
t = 1	200,000	0.8850	177,000
t = 2	100,000	0.7831	78,310
t = 3	100,000	0.6931	69,310
t = 4	500,000	0.6133	306,650
		Total	231,270

Since the NPV is positive the decision to make in-house is confirmed.

Activity 6.2

Listen to Audio Programme 2, 'Project appraisal', in which a company's managers discuss the pros and cons of a make or buy decision from the production, marketing and strategic points of view, as well as from a financial perspective.

6.3 ORGANISATIONAL GROWTH V. GROWTH BY ACQUISITION

This final sub-section forms a link between Unit 5 and Unit 6. In a sense the concept of organisational growth v. growth by acquisition can be equated to the 'make or buy' decision, as discussed in the previous sub-section. We can compare the 'make' decision to internal growth, i.e. expanding internal facilities, shops, hotel rooms and so on; and the 'buy' decision with the (outside) acquisition of these facilities. Management will essentially have to go through a similar thought process to arrive at a decision either to grow internally or by acquisition. However, the capital outlay for acquiring a company (and it has to be paid in advance) is nearly always much larger than internal expansion, where the capital outlay can usually be spread over a period of time. This in turn means that a plan to acquire another business has a major impact and thus requires a great deal of extra management time and analysis in the investment decision-making process.

The concept of internal v. external growth is illustrated in the case study in Box 6.2. These specific acquisitions are often of the 'horizontal' type, which usually means taking over a competitor who sells the same type of product or operates in a similar market. In a sense the decisions to make these acquisitions are of a CAPEX nature, because the firm does not spend capital to expand existing in-house facilities but has selected to purchase facilities from outside as a going concern.

The case study briefly describes the acquisition of the Waterstone's chain of bookshops by W.H. Smith. The case illustrates the concept of 'make or buy', as applied to the retail environment and shows that the company was successful in 'buying' (acquiring) a book retail brand name, in the broadest sense, rather then developing over time their own specialist book retail brand (organic growth in-house), e.g. the Sherratt & Hughes shops (an existing division of W.H. Smith).

BOX 6.2   CASE STUDY: W.H. SMITH INVESTMENT IN WATERSTONE'S

During 1989 the Waterstone's chain of bookstores was acquired by W.H. Smith. It was decided to merge the stores with the Smiths' owned Sherratt & Hughes (S&H) chain and to form a 78-shop chain which would trade under the Waterstone's name. This would be the largest specialist book shop in the UK. The Waterstone's brand name conveys a passion for books and Smith's management felt that the brand name would position them in the market for the high-spending, discerning book buyer. The major reason for the acquisition and the merger with S&H was that the 'in-house' development of a brand name with the same perceived qualities as Waterstone's would simply take too long.

During 1993, the book market in the UK showed very little growth in real terms, but Waterstone's increased its total sales by 19%. This performance easily out-distanced that of any significant competitor in this segment of the market.

The W.H. Smith 1996 annual report stated that Waterstone's had increased its turnover to £169.2 m, up by 14.1% from the previous period. Operating profit had reached £12.8m, up 47.1%. The return on capital employed increased from 3.7% to 9.0%.

The company claimed that Waterstone's strength lay in its booksellers, who are passionate about what they do, throughout the 100 stores in the chain. The company intended to add another 26 stores over the three years from 1997.

The success of the acquisition enabled W.H. Smith and Waterstone's to achieve a 25% share of the UK book market by 1996.

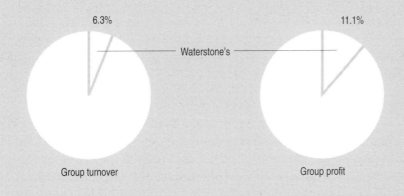

Figure 6.1   Waterstone's contribution to the turnover and profit of W.H. Smith

Finally, after the above case of the acquisitions by W.H. Smith and their plans for expansion of the Waterstone division, it is interesting to note the transitory nature of business and large companies.

STOP PRESS: WATERSTONE'S IN DILLONS LINK

W.H. Smith is poised to sell its Waterstone's book chain for about £300million to a joint venture between EMI and Advent International, a venture capital company.

The deal, which is expected to be announced later this week, will result in the creation of a new retailing group including Waterstone's and the EMI-owned Dillons bookstores [one of the largest chains in the UK] and HMV record shops.

The company will be chaired by Tim Waterstone, founder of the book chain [he sold the book chain to W.H. Smith in 1989, see above case study]. Mr. Waterstone had a take-over bid for the whole of W.H. Smith rebuffed by the company last autumn, but succeeded in forcing W.H. Smith into a strategic U-turn. W.H. Smith has also put its Virgin/Our Price music chain and The Wall, its US music business, up for sale in order to concentrate on its core 400 stores.

The new EMI retailing group will also incorporate Daisy and Tom, the children's clothing and toy store recently established by Mr Waterstone.

EMI is believed to be keen to take the group public eventually. HMV has about 330 outlets, and Waterstone's has 120 stores.

Source: *The Times*, 23 February, 1998

In conclusion, we must note that the major task which faces managers in the acquisition decision-making process is to determine a value for the company they want to take over. While in this Unit we have dealt with a range of issues in the CAPEX process, Unit 6 is devoted to the subject of company valuation, which is inextricably related to the CAPEX process. However, the subject of company appraisal is complex and the decision to take over another firm has major implications for the acquiring organisation.

SUMMARY

In this section, we have illustrated the issues surrounding the shortage of investment capital to which most, if not all, organisations are subject most of the time. Capital rationing issues involve the selection of an optimal array of investment projects under financial and other resource constraints. We made the distinction between hard and soft capital rationing.

We have discussed the aspect of competing projects and the make or buy decision, where an organisation has the opportunity to outsource its production or services instead of the internal creation of their products. The section also dealt with the investment choice organisations must make in the case of competing projects. In order to illustrate this concept we provided a numerical example, which showed one of the selection methods management can apply in their decision-making process. While this section has concentrated on the financial aspects, it is essential for decisions to be taken in light of their non-financial and strategic implications.

Finally, we briefly discussed the choice of internal organisational growth v. growth by acquisition. We compared this to the 'make or buy' decision, except that the capital outlay to 'buy' is in most cases many times larger than to 'make'.

7 ACE COMPANY: SPREADSHEET EXERCISE

The case study, based on ACE Company, consists of a relatively complex project proposal. Students are required to answer the two main questions at the end of the case, which are self-explanatory. The use of Excel is recommended in order to solve the quantitative element of the questions. In addition to achieving the skills to prepare project cash flow profiles, by the use of spreadsheets, and arriving at a reasonable conclusion to the financial appraisal, you are encouraged to support their conclusion with qualitative information. This case helps to develop your understanding of the importance of strategic considerations in capital budgeting decisions, as well as how to incorporate such considerations into your analysis.

7.1 INTRODUCTION

This hypothetical case uses the development of a new product to introduce a strategic dimension to the teaching of capital budgeting. We suggest that you consider such factors as the cannibalisation of an existing profitable product and the possibility of deterring competitors' entry into the market. The case exercise begins with a simple NPV analysis of the decision without considering the potential impact on competitors' actions. Then it progresses to increasing layers of complexity which introduce the strategic aspects of the decision. This process is intended to enhance your mastery of capital budgeting methods. It also helps you to appreciate that effective management requires going beyond the learning of techniques to consider the larger, competitive context.

You may wish to revise the discussion of NPV in Section 4.3.1 of *Vital Statistics*.

7.2 EXERCISE

ACE Company is the technology and market leader in the portable electronic games industry. The company is currently very successful with its Model X, which has been on the market for several years. ACE's management believe that because of increased competition from other types of entertainment, the demand for Model X will dry up after three more years. The company has forecast Model X's net cash inflows in the next three years to be £400 million, £300 million, and £200 million, respectively.

7.3 NEW PRODUCT DEVELOPMENT

ACE's senior managers are considering the development and introduction of a replacement for Model X, to be called Model Z. According to the engineers, ACE already possesses the technical expertise to develop Model Z. However, the earliest that this product can be introduced into the market is one year from now, as it will take this long to develop and test the new product, co-ordinate with suppliers for parts, set up the production process, and arrange for other related activities. The total cost of these development activities is estimated at £550 million.

All of ACE's top managers agree that Model Z's market potential in terms of net cash inflow would be £200 million in year 2, £400 million in year 3, £300 million in year 4, and £100 million in year 5. They also agree that Model Z would maintain ACE's leadership position in the portable electronic games industry.

Management expect that, in addition to developing its own customer base, Model Z also would draw some sales away from Model X. The expected amount of this 'cannibalisation' is £100 million of net cash inflows per year. Table 7.1 summarises ACE's prediction of net cash flows for the next five years, for Model X by itself and with the introduction of Model Z at the end of year 1 (in effect the beginning of year 2). For simplicity, cash outflows are assumed to occur at the beginning of the year while cash inflows are assumed to occur at the year-end. Thus, for example, the £550 million development cost in year 1 is assumed to occur at time 0, while the net cash inflow from introducing Model Z at the beginning of year 2 is assumed to occur at the end of that year. Also note that in the table, net cash inflows of £100 million per year are shifted from Model X to Model Z in years 2 and 3.

Table 7.1 Model X, introducing Model Z at end of year 1 (£m)				
		After one year		
Year	**Model X only**	**Model X**	**Model Z**	**Total**
0	0	0	(550)	(550)
1	400	400	0	400
2	300	200*	300*	500
3	200	100*	500*	600
4	0	0	300	300
5	0	0	100	100

Reflects £100m cannibalisation of Model X by Model Z

Management have decided that the development expenditure, should the project go ahead, will be capitalised over the life of the project.

ACE's after-tax cost of capital is 10 %. The development costs would attract a 25% writing down allowance, based on the reducing balance method, for taxation purposes. The corporate tax rate is 35%, payable one year after year-end.

7.4 EXTENDING THE DEVELOPMENT PERIOD FOR MODEL Z

Several members of top management are concerned about Model Z's erosion of Model X sales. They propose that it would be better to spread the development of Model Z over two years and to introduce it at the beginning of year 3 instead of year 2. They suggest that this plan has two major advantages: (1) it would avoid the £100 million erosion in Model X's net cash inflows in year 2; and (2) the engineers have projected that extending the time for the development process will yield substantial savings due to efficiencies in scheduling. They have estimated that the two-year plan would reduce Model Z's total development cost to £300 million. Half of this total would be spent in each of the two years.

Table 7.2 summarises the estimated net cash flows for the two-year plan. Compared with the one-year plan, Model X's year 2 net cash inflow is higher by £100 million. This is because cannibalisation by Model Z in year 2 is avoided.

Table 7.2 Introducing Model Z over two years (£m)			
		After two Years	
Year	Model X only	Model X	Model Z	Total
0	0	0	(150)	(150)
1	400	400	(150)	250
2	300	300	0	300
3	200	100*	500*	600
4	0	0	300	300
5	0	0	100	100

Reflects £100m cannibalisation of Model X by Model Z.

Proponents of the two-year plan acknowledge that delaying Model Z's introduction by one year would require forgoing its year 2 £300 million net cash inflow. They emphasise that this sacrifice is more than made up by the additional £100 million cash inflow from Model X in year 2 and the £250 million savings in Model Z development costs.

7.5 OTHER CONSIDERATIONS

Supporters of the one-year plan argue that proponents of the two-year plan have overlooked a major factor: that the timing of Model Z's introduction could have an impact on competitors' actions. They maintain that if ACE does not introduce Model Z as quickly as possible, ACE's major competitor would most certainly enter the market with a comparable product. In response to a query from these managers, ACE's engineers have conducted a study of the competitor's current capabilities. They have reported that due to the competitor's less sophisticated technologies, it will require two years to develop a comparable product for market introduction.

The nature of the industry is such that there is a significant 'first mover' advantage. Similar products that reach the market at the same time tend to get equal shares of the market. Once a product is introduced, it tends to get so entrenched that comparable products subsequently introduced can gain only insignificant market shares.

Activity 7.1

(i) Using NPV computations, analyse the one-year and two-year development alternatives. At this time, ignore the potential introduction of a comparable product by ACE's major competitor. Which alternative would you recommend?

(ii) How would you modify your analysis in (i) to address the potential introduction of a competing product by ACE's major competitor?

 We have supplied three files on disk for you to use in this Activity. They are CAPX, CAPXACEA and CAPXACEB.

SUMMARY AND CONCLUSIONS

In this section we pull together the topics discussed in this unit and summarise their impact on project appraisal procedures, as practised in a range of organisations, linking these practices to the topics in this and other units of B821.

In this unit, we have attempted to introduce you to many aspects of capital investment decision-making. Although you may have acquired a knowledge of some of the topics in your previous studies, we tried to amalgamate the wide range of theories and issues which underpin the subject of CAPEX. Organisational strategy appears to be the skeleton on which the whole process of capital decision-making is based, in that a stated or implied mission statement drives the needs for the investment in capital facilities. We then narrowed our discussion to the techniques of investment appraisal, by examining capital budgeting theories, their strengths and weaknesses. The examination of specific appraisal issues explained some of the underlying theoretical inconsistencies in the application of DCF techniques. Inflation and taxation were examined only in so far as they are linked to CAPEX, because in reality these subjects are too comprehensive to be discussed in their entirety in this course. Due to the fact that many organisations have operations in a number of countries, we looked at CAPEX processes within the international environment.

We discussed risk issues in the capital expenditure context, since expenditure in long-term projects inevitably involves risks. We also explored the options approach to capital investment, which is a relatively novel approach to the process of CAPEX decision-making. This development is a valuable tool enabling organisations to manage risk.

We considered the funding of capital projects and the importance of the financing decision on the overall capital structure, building on the issues described in Unit 4. Leasing is an important finance mechanism for a range of plant and equipment investments, and the description and examples have hopefully added to your understanding of this subject. Project finance was discussed in some depth, as this type of financing vehicle is becoming increasingly popular as a method for funding large capital projects, such as power stations, oil refineries, etc. The opportunities and complexities of project finance were described in a case study illustrating the investment in a liquid gas facility in Oman. We also introduced and explained the Private Finance Initiative (PFI), which is providing public-sector organisations in the UK with a means of tapping into private-sector financial resources for funding their projects.

Although capital rationing has already been discussed in Units 1 and 2, we revisited it in the context of CAPEX. Nearly all organisations are subject to cash and other constraints and managers often have to choose between competing projects.

You should now have achieved the following learning objectives and should:

- appreciate how organisations implement their capital appraisal procedures

- recognise the wide range of issues involved in capital investment decisions
- assess the strategic implications of investing in capital equipment and facilities
- be able to apply a range of project appraisal methods to various types of projects and organisations in which CAPEX decisions are made
- appreciate the importance of, and the problems of identifying and measuring, risk in the context of capital investment decision-making
- understand the problems and opportunities of raising funds for capital projects in the market-place
- be able to undertake the investment appraisal exercise at the end of this unit.

ANSWERS TO EXERCISES

Exercise 3.1 _____

From Unit 1 we know that:

$(1 + R) = (1 + r)(1 + \text{expected inflation rate})$

where

R = nominal interest rate

r = real interest rate

In this example, R = 10% and r = 3%

Expected inflation rate = $\frac{1.10}{1.03}$ = 1.068 or 6.8%

If nominal sales growth is assumed to 5% per year, and expected inflation is 6.8%, we can say:

$(1 + \text{nominal growth rate}) = (1 + \text{real growth rate})(1 + \text{expected inflation rate})$

$1.05 = (1 + g)(1.068)$

$g = \frac{1.05}{1.068} - 1 = -0.0168 = -1.7\%$

So, although nominal sales growth looks good, the projected sales growth is actually less than the inflation rate.

Exercise 4.1 _____

State	NPV (£)		Probability		(£)
Boom	+769.4	×	0.1	=	+76.9
Normal	+476.3	×	0.3	=	+142.9
Depressed	−291.5	×	0.6	=	−174.9
				ENPV	+44.9

The Paraiso project is still worth while under the changed probability assumptions.

REFERENCES AND SUGGESTED READING

Blaxhill, M.F. and Hout, T.M. (1991) *Harvard Business Review*, July–August.

Brealey, R.A. and Myers, S.C.(1996) *Principles of Corporate Finance*, McGraw-Hill.

Buckley, A. (1998) *International Capital Budgeting*, Prentice Hall.

Buckley, A. and Tse, K. (1996) 'Real operating options and foreign direct investment: a synthetic approach', *European Management Journal*, No.3, pp. 304–314.

Collins, D. (1997) '4P's', *Public Money and Management*, July–September.

Dixit, A.K. and Pindyck, R.S. (1995) 'The options approach to capital investment', *Harvard Business Review*, May–June, pp. 105–115.

Drury, C. and Tayles, M. (1997) 'The misapplication of capital investment appraisal techniques', *Management Decision*, No.2, pp. 86–93.

HM Treasury (1995) 'Private opportunity, public benefit', published by *The London Financial News*, 28 July–3 August.

Ho, S.M. and Pike, R.H. (1991) 'The use of risk analysis techniques in capital investment appraisal', *Accounting and Business Research*, Vol. 21, No. 83, pp. 227–38.

Lessard, D.R. (1996) 'Incorporating country risk in the valuation of offshore projects', *Journal of Applied Corporate Finance*, Fall, pp. 52–63.

LEX Column, *Financial Times*, 7 July, 1997.

London Transport (1996/7) *Annual Report and Accounts*.

Lumijärvi, O.P. (1992) 'Selling of capital investment to top management', *Management Accounting Research,* No.2, pp.171–88.

Lumby, S. (1995) *Investment Appraisal and Financial Decisions*, Chapman and Hall.

Maccarone, P. (1996) 'Organising the capital budgeting process in large firms', *Management Decision*, No.6, pp.43–56.

Murray, A. (1985) *Great Financial Disasters*, Arthur Barker Ltd.

Nevitt, D. (1989) 'Project Finance', *Euromoney.*

Nevitt and Fabozzi (1996) 'Project Finance', *Euromoney.*

Northcott, D. (1992) *Capital Investment Decision Making*, Academic Press.

Pike, R.H. (1996) 'A longitudinal survey on capital budgeting practices', *Journal of Business Finance & Accounting*, January pp.79–92.

Samuels, J.M., Wilkes, F.M. and Brayshaw, R.E. (1995) *Management of Company Finance*, Chapman and Hall.

Wilkes, F.M., Samuels, J.M. and Greenfield, S.M. (1996) 'Investment decision making in UK manufacturing industry', *Management Decision*, No.4, pp. 62–71.

ACKNOWLEDGEMENTS

Grateful acknowledgement is made to the following sources for permission to reproduce material in this unit:

Text

p. 40–41: Lumby, S. 1994, *Investment Appraisal and Financial Decisions,* Fifth edition, pp. 535–536, International Thomson Publishing Services Ltd; pp. 71–74: adapted from Chow, C. W., Hwang, Y. and Togo, D. F. 1995, 'The case study of ACE: a case for incorporating complex situations into the teaching of Capital Budgeting', *Issues in Accounting Education,* **10**(2), American Accounting Association.

Figures

Figure 1.1: 'A Universal Model of the CI Decision-making Activity?' from Northcott, D. 1992, *Capital Investment Decision Making,* Academic Press, International Thomson Publishing Services Ltd; *Figure 2.1:* Maccarone, P. 1996, 'Organizing the Capital Budgeting Process in Large Firms', *Management Design,* **6**, MCB University Press Ltd; *Figures 5.1 and 5.2:* 'Private Financial Initiative – PFI', *Public Service Management,* September 1996, Chartered Institute of Management Accountants; *Figure 5.3:* Buckley, A. 1996, *International Capital Budgeting,* Prentice-Hall UK Ltd.

Tables

Tables 3.1, 3.2 and 3.3: Drury, C. and Tayles, M. 1997, 'The Misapplication of Capital Investment Appraisal Techniques', *Management Decision,* **2**, MCB University Press Ltd; *Table 4.1:* Ho, S.M. and Pike, R.H. 1991, 'Risk Analysis in Capital Budgeting Contexts: Simple or Sophisticated', *Accounting and Business Research,* **21**(83), pp. 227–238, by permission of R.H. Pike; *Table 5.1:* Lessard, D.R. 1996, 'Incorporating Country Risk in the Valuation of Offshore Projects', *Journal of Applied Corporate Finance,* **9**(3), Stern Stewart Management Services, Inc.; *Tables 7.1 and 7.2:* Chow, C.W., Hwang, Y. and Togo, D.F. 1995, 'The case study of ACE: a case for incorporating complex situations into the teaching of Capital Budgeting', *Issues in Accounting Education,* **10**(2), American Accounting Association.

Illustrations

p. 16: Copyright © London Regional Transport; p. 43: Roger Beale, from the *Financial Times;* p. 53: ALB, *International Freighting Weekly,* 20 August 1987; p. 55: Shell International; p. 68: Peter Muller.

Every effort has been made to trace copyright owners, but if any has been inadvertently overlooked, the publishers will be pleased to make the necessary arrangements at the first opportunity.

B821 FINANCIAL STRATEGY